The Silent Abuse

Sherry Lou Canino

Dedication

This book is dedicated to my son, Elias Gabriel Hibbard. He has been my greatest gift and blessing, my biggest cheerleader, and a constant source of inspiration and support. There is truly no greater love than a mother's love for her child.

To all the survivors of narcissistic abuse who have suffered and are still suffering, I see you, I hear you, and you, too, can heal.

Acknowledgments

Writing this book has been one of the hardest things ever. It has brought up deep pain from my past that I'd blocked out and forgotten, yet it has also provided some of the most healing moments on my journey of recovery from a lifetime of narcissistic abuse. To Alex, who has sat with me through the telling of my story, chapter by chapter, and been such a kind and gentle soul throughout, I cannot express how much your care and kindness have meant to me.

I am deeply grateful to my spiritual mentor, Kasia Kulbowksa, and my energy worker, Jennifer Currie, who have held space for me, witnessed my tears and guided me with such compassion throughout this multi-year healing process. I wrote this book to be a voice for narcissistic abuse survivors who have not been able to share their stories or feel like their voices aren't being heard.

This journey has been an emotional roller coaster, yet the best ride I've ever experienced. To James and the team, thank you for always being there and helping articulate my words in such a raw and honest way.

About the Author

Sherry Canino was born and raised in the charming town of Baldwinsville, Central New York, where she grew up as the youngest of eight siblings. With three sisters and four brothers, her upbringing was filled with a rich blend of family life. Sherry earned her degree in accounting and dedicated over 20 years to a successful career in the field. Her passion for art also led her to run a thriving art business, which earned her recognition in Syracuse Women's Magazine. She further enriched her career by facilitating art therapy groups for individuals with eating disorders, a cause close to her heart.

Preface

Writing a book is often challenging and revealing. This book is the culmination of years of reflection, deep introspection, and an unwavering desire to help others find their own strength. At its core, it is a story about survival—about what it means to endure emotional abuse that leaves no visible scars but creates profound emotional wounds.

For many years, I found myself lost in my own experiences, unable to name my struggles. Growing up in an environment where the dynamics were emotionally charged and abusive, my understanding of love, care, and family became skewed. I spent years trying to make sense of the experiences that shaped my view of relationships, struggling to reconcile the version of my reality manipulated and controlled by those closest to me.

The lessons I learned through those experiences were harsh and difficult. It took decades for me to unravel the impact of growing up in an emotionally toxic environment. For years, I failed to recognize the patterns repeating themselves, not just in my childhood home but also in my adult relationships. The constant pursuit of love and validation led me into the arms of partners who treated me similarly to those early experiences—partners whose affection was as conditional and fleeting as I had known growing up.

This book is not just a recounting of the past but a message of hope for those who may still be struggling. It's for those trying to understand why they keep finding themselves in the same situations, drawn to relationships that cause pain yet feel familiar. It's for those ready to confront their trauma, acknowledge its presence, and begin the healing process.

I want to acknowledge that healing is not a linear process. It comes in waves—sometimes progress is made, and other times, it feels like you're taking steps backward. There are days when the weight of the past feels too heavy, but with persistence, it is possible to move forward. In my journey, I have found that sharing my story has helped me heal and offer comfort to others in similar situations. The goal is to provide a voice for those who feel silenced to speak openly about experiences that many find too difficult to articulate.

The hardest part of my journey has been coming to terms with the reality of my upbringing and the relationships I pursued. Realizing that the love I had known was conditional—based on meeting impossible standards and manipulated to maintain control—was a difficult truth to accept. It required me to unlearn years of conditioning and to start understanding my worth beyond the roles others had assigned to me.

Writing this book has not been easy. There were times when reliving these experiences felt like opening old wounds, but it also allowed me to put into words the emotions I had buried for so long. It was peeling back layers, confronting my fears, and making sense of what had once seemed beyond comprehension. And, perhaps most importantly, it was a process of letting go—of releasing the hold that the past had over me and choosing to see myself not as a victim but as someone who has endured, survived, and emerged stronger.

To anyone who picks up this book and sees a reflection of their own experiences, I hope you find comfort in knowing that you are not alone. The emotional scars we carry may not be visible, but they are real, and they deserve to be acknowledged. The healing journey is deeply personal, and there is no right or wrong way to move forward. What matters is the decision to take that first step, to no longer remain in the shadows of your pain but to face it and rise above it.

As I share my journey, I want to make it clear that this is not a book of easy answers or quick solutions. It is not about sweeping resolutions or miraculous recoveries. Instead, it is about the strength in vulnerability, the courage it takes to speak the truth, and the resilience within each of us. Healing is an ongoing journey—one that requires patience, compassion, and the willingness to confront uncomfortable truths.

To all the survivors who read these pages, I see you. I hear you. I hope that, in my words, you find an understanding of what you have been through and the strength to continue your journey toward healing. Though the road may be difficult, there is always hope for a future free from the shadows of the past—a future where you can embrace who you are and know that you are enough

Contents

Chapter 1: The Youngest of Eight- Growing Up in Chaos

I woke up one morning and didn't recognize myself. This realization encapsulates much of my childhood experience, growing up as the youngest of eight children in a bustling household. Being the youngest often meant I was considered the "golden child," a term my siblings used half-jokingly. From an early age, I found myself in a unique position where even my older siblings sought my advice. They believed that if I asked our parents for something, it was more likely to be granted, and most of the time, they were right.

This dynamic shaped much of my early life. I became hyper-vigilant, always alert to the moods and needs of those around me. This heightened awareness made me very careful in how I approached people and situations. I developed a tactful and charismatic way of interacting that allowed me to get what I wanted, not just from my parents but from people in general. Whether it was at school, with friends, or in other social settings, I learned how to read the room, understand what people wanted, and present my requests in a way that made them hard to refuse.

My ability to influence others was seen as a natural talent, and I often became the spokesperson for my siblings when it came to negotiating with our parents. If we wanted a later bedtime, permission to go out, or a new toy, I was usually the one to make the request. My siblings trusted that I had the best chance of success, and I took this responsibility seriously.

While I excelled in negotiating for my siblings, my home life was far from ideal. Although I didn't witness my dad physically abusing my mom, we, as kids, often heard their fights. The house would transform into a storm, with their shouts as thunderclaps. Whenever the storm began, we knew what to do: either retreat to our rooms and lock the doors or, if possible, escape outside to get away from the chaos. It was an unspoken rule that when their arguments started, we vanished to any place that felt safe.

My mom often opened up to me about the fights, showing me the bruises on her arms left by my dad. These heart-wrenching conversations were confusing and distressing for me as a child. Even though I didn't see much of the violence firsthand, the stories and physical evidence etched a permanent scar on my understanding of family and conflict, a scar that would never fade.

One of my earliest memories is from when I was just two years old. With eight kids in the house, space was always tight, and my crib was in my parents' bedroom. The room was small and crowded, evidence of the bustling life of a large family. One night, I was awakened by the sound of my parents fighting. The hallway light cast long shadows into the room, and even at that age, I could sense the tension in the air. The loud voices and angry tones created a frightening atmosphere, one that was all too familiar in our household.

My oldest sister, Carol, came into the bedroom, took me out of my crib, and dressed me in shoes and a little jacket over my pajamas. Her actions were swift and purposeful, showing her understanding of handling such situations. She carried me past our parents, who were caught in a heated argument. My siblings were very adamant that my dad had something held to my mom's throat, possibly a knife or screwdriver. This incident highlighted the chaotic environment in which we lived and the protective role my older siblings often had to play.

This was my very first experience with narcissistic abuse at the age of two, although I didn't understand it at the time. Narcissistic abuse often involves reactive abuse, where the abuser provokes the victim through yelling, saying hurtful things, or other actions to elicit a reaction. It's important to understand that the reaction is not abusive but a response to ongoing provocation. The abuser continues these actions to get the other person to "react." This in itself is the abuse. As Dr. John Gottman explains, *"The victim is never the abuser in these situations."* Understanding this distinction is crucial because it sheds light on the true nature of the abuse and the dynamics at play.

These experiences contributed to the surge of anxiety and dread I often felt when my dad came home from work, as his arrival frequently marked the beginning of conflicts. As young kids, we didn't fully understand what triggered these arguments, but we could feel a shift in the atmosphere the moment he walked through the door. The tension was almost unbearable, knowing that my mom's complaints could escalate into heated exchanges at any moment. My mom would start complaining and yelling about various grievances, and sometimes, these exchanges would intensify. My dad, a quiet man by nature, would try to remain calm, but eventually, he would reach a breaking point. He might yell, throw a dish, or simply walk away. Sometimes, he would leave the house entirely, and on occasion, my mom would follow him, continuing the argument outside.

My mom often did things that would provoke my dad to come after me when I was younger. One instance was when I twisted my ankle during indoor track practice. I still wanted to go to the meet to cheer my team on, but my mom got mad and didn't want me to go. The situation escalated into a big argument. My sister Sue and I were upstairs in our bedroom when we heard my dad coming. We quickly removed the screen from the upstairs window, climbed out, and scrambled down the tree. We ran into the nearby woods before he broke down our bedroom door. These moments of fear and escape were a regular part of our lives, and they taught us to be resourceful and to rely on each other.

The volatility at home was a constant, but my understanding of it evolved over time. My dad's abusive behavior toward my mom and us kids was a pervasive part of our household, but not all of us experienced it in the same way. It wasn't until recently that I realized my mom was a narcissist, constantly picking at my dad and causing him to react. She had a way of pushing his buttons, which would lead to explosive outbursts. This realization shifted my perspective on their relationship and the dynamics within our family. My mom's behavior wasn't just a response to my dad's abuse; it was often the catalyst for it. This toxic cycle made our home a battlefield, with each of us caught in the crossfire.

The emotional and physical abuse extended beyond my father. My mom had a habit of slapping us across the face whenever she didn't like something we did or said. I remember being as young as five and getting slapped because I didn't want her to buy me a dress for kindergarten—I wanted to wear pants. This kind of physical punishment was a regular occurrence, reinforcing a sense of fear and helplessness. She frequently spoke negatively about my sister Candy, my brother Danny, and my brother Terry. It seemed like she hated them, or at least wanted us to believe that she did, casting them as villains in her personal drama.

In stark contrast, one of my brothers was my mom's favorite son among all the boys. Although I was considered the golden child and enjoyed a special status, her favoritism toward him was undeniable. My mom absolutely adored him, and he could do no wrong in her eyes. This blatant favoritism only fueled the resentment and jealousy among us. While Mark enjoyed her undivided love and attention, the rest of us were left to navigate the emotional minefield she created. Her favoritism was yet another tool she used to manipulate and control us, deepening the divides within our family.

As I grew older, I noticed these patterns in my own relationships. While I didn't start arguments the way my mom did, I found myself reacting similarly when I felt unheard. If someone didn't listen to me, I would follow them or raise my voice, trying to get my point across. It was an unconscious mimicry of the behaviors I had witnessed so many times in my childhood. Research by Dr. John Gottman, a leading psychologist in relationship studies, supports this observation, indicating that early family dynamics influence adult conflict resolution styles.

The influence of these early family dynamics became even more apparent when significant changes occurred in our household. At the age of 10, my father decided to start his own business. Whether things improved overall is uncertain; financially, they probably did, but the beginning was stressful in a different way. We all had to pitch in, doing various tasks for the business. It was a new kind of pressure that we hadn't experienced before. The house, once a place of family gatherings and shared meals, turned into a makeshift office where everyone had a role. As we got older, there was a lot of jealousy among my siblings about who was working in the business and who wasn't. This tension simmered beneath the surface, creating an undercurrent of resentment.

Some of my sisters wanted to work in the business, but they never told my parents. I found this out later, and it explained a lot of the jealousy that had built up over the years. They felt left out and excluded, watching their siblings take part in something they believed they had a right to be involved in. My mother, who had always been a stay-at-home mom, eventually went to work in the office. She did this when I was around 14. She hated working and was miserable all the time. Her unhappiness was palpable, and she came home at the end of the day, always in a bad mood. This period was one of the worst summers of my life growing up.

During this time, all I thought about was killing myself. I hated being around her and being home; it was pure awful. My sister and I were also working in the office at that time because my mom said we had to, so it was like being with her 24 hours a day. The constant proximity to her negativity and frustration made life unbearable. There was no escape from her complaints and the oppressive atmosphere she created. One night, things must have been terrible. My sister and I were the only ones home, and I grabbed a kitchen knife, intending to kill myself. My sister grabbed the knife out of my hand and stopped me. I was so mad at her for doing so, but looking back. I realize she saved my life.

Later, when I was 21, I worked closely with my mom as a secretary and did accounting for my parents' business. One day, she made a mistake on some forms. I tried repeatedly to explain the correct way to her, but she became frustrated and started yelling at me, insisting that I was wrong. My dad came over and asked what was going on. When I explained, he took my mom's side. When I didn't agree with him, he got angry and started punching my stomach, pinning me against the wall. One of my brothers came out of his office and pulled my dad off me. In the struggle, my dad got cut by his own glasses. Later, my mom yelled at me for hurting my father, completely ignoring the fact that he had been the one to attack me.

My mom just complained about anything and everything we did or didn't do. It went on and on every single day, a relentless barrage of criticism and negativity. As author Brene Brown says, *"Staying vulnerable is a risk we have to take if we want to experience connection."* Reflecting on this quote, I realize how much vulnerability was suppressed in my household. Despite the constant turmoil, I've learned that embracing vulnerability is essential for true connection.

In recognizing this, I'm now working on breaking the dysfunctional cycle and striving for healthier, more authentic connections in my own life.

Chapter 2: The Golden Child's Burden

In narcissistic family systems, landing the role of the "golden child" is like winning a twisted family lottery – a ticket to special treatment, but with a hefty price tag of manipulation and unrealistic expectations. The golden child is showered with special attention and adoration, not out of genuine love or appreciation, but to serve the narcissistic parent's insatiable need for admiration and control. This child becomes the family's shining star, often idealized and paraded as a symbol of perfection, while the other siblings are left in the shadows. This setup creates a toxic environment where favoritism is the norm, and the golden child's so-called "perfection" is a tool for the narcissistic parent's grandiosity. Dr. Karyl McBride's book *Will I Ever Be Good Enough?* Goes into these dynamics, shedding light on the damaging effects of narcissistic parenting and the roles assigned to children in such families.

In my family, I somehow managed to snag the coveted role of the golden child. Compared to my siblings, I faced fewer consequences for my actions. While they were punished harshly for minor mistakes, I was often let off the hook or even praised. My mother always spoke highly of me, emphasizing how smart and capable I was. This constant praise was part of a larger strategy to maintain control and manipulate our family dynamics. It also served to isolate me from my siblings, who viewed me with a mix of envy and resentment.

My birthday was always a major event in our household, especially considering it was just four days before Christmas. My mom would wrap my gifts weeks in advance, displaying them prominently where everyone could see them. She would make a special cake of my choice, turning my birthday into a grand celebration. Meanwhile, my brother, whose birthday was two days after Christmas, often received far less attention. I remember he would get candles stuck in leftover pie, highlighting the disparity in treatment.

This favoritism was evident to my siblings, who believed I was treated better. When I was young, they always loved me, but as I got older, they became resentful of me. They saw the preferential treatment I received and felt overlooked and undervalued, leading to tension and conflict. However, the truth is more nuanced. My mother's high regard for me was part of her triangulation tactics. She wanted to create jealousy and competition among us, keeping the family divided and ensuring her control remained unchallenged. By appearing to favor me, she manipulated our perceptions and nurtured discord. This manipulation ensured that our focus remained on competing for her approval rather than uniting against her controlling behavior. It also kept us emotionally dependent on her validation.

The effects of this dynamic extended beyond my relationship with my siblings and deeply impacted my relationship with my father. My mother's manipulative tactics created a complicated and often strained dynamic between us. While she encouraged us to love our father when he was present, she would speak negatively about him when he was not around, portraying him as a villain. This contradictory behavior left me feeling confused and uncertain about my relationship with him. As a result, I often felt torn between a desire to be close to my father and a conflicting sense of loyalty to my mother. This confusion was compounded by my deeper, more complicated resentment toward him. Even as young as 7 or 8, I would ask my mom, "Why don't we just leave Dad?" In my eyes, if he was so bad for her, then staying didn't make sense. But her response—usually about how she couldn't support us on her own—set a contradictory example that stuck with me. On one hand, she always told me, "NEVER depend on a man; have your own money." Yet, in practice, she stayed in an unhealthy marriage, which planted the belief that staying with an abusive partner might somehow be necessary for security. This conflicting message haunted me, later surfacing in my own relationship with my husband.

One of the most uncomfortable aspects of my visits as a young adult was when my mother would criticize my father right in front of him. It created an incredibly awkward atmosphere, leaving me feeling torn and uneasy. I remember one instance when my mother claimed she caught my dad cheating on her. She said she found him at a restaurant with another woman. Given that this was supposedly before I was born, and knowing that my mother didn't drive until I was around four or five years old, I strongly believe this story was a fabrication, a means of gaslighting him and us. This tactic was used to maintain her narrative and control, further isolating my father and making us doubt his character. These fabrications created an environment of mistrust and instability in our household.

Despite the negative narrative my mother tried to create, I had moments where I connected deeply with my father. One of the most memorable periods was when I was in the eighth grade and joined the varsity indoor track team. My coach asked me to run because I was quite good, and my mom agreed to let me participate. My dad took on the responsibility of picking me up from the late-night meets, which sometimes ended as late as 11 p.m. or midnight. These long rides home became a cherished time for us to talk and bond. He even started coming early to watch me run, something I had always wished for but never expected to happen. As author Mitch Albom once said, *"Sometimes when you sacrifice something precious, you're not really losing it. You're just passing it on to someone else."* These moments gave me a sense of normalcy and joy, away from the tense atmosphere at home. During these times, I felt truly supported and loved by my father.

The time spent with my dad during those rides home was deeply meaningful and unforgettable to me. Seeing him there, cheering me on, made me feel valued and loved. I had friends whose fathers were always present, and I longed for that same experience. Finally, having my dad show up for me meant the world to me, and it strengthened our relationship. It gave me a glimpse of what a healthy parent-child relationship could be like, which was completely different from my interactions with my mother. These experiences became cherished memories that I held onto, especially during difficult times.

However, my mother soon noticed our growing closeness and became jealous. One evening, she accused me of keeping my dad out too late and being selfish, claiming that he needed his rest for work. She told me that unless I could find another way to get home, I would have to quit the team. This was devastating news, but thankfully, my coach stepped in and offered to drive me home, even though it was out of his way. His kindness allowed me to stay on the team and maintain my relationship with my father. This intervention by my coach was a lifeline that prevented my mother from completely severing my connection with my dad. It also showed me that there were people who cared about my well-being outside of my immediate family.

Once, during a quiet moment alone with my dad, I apologized for the late pickups. He responded, "Baby girl," a term of endearment he used only when we were alone, "You know how your mom gets mad about things. We just have to do things to make her happy." His words were a bittersweet acknowledgment of the situation. They highlighted his understanding of my mother's behavior and his willingness to manage it for the sake of our relationship. This conversation left a lasting impression on me, emphasizing the need for compromise and sacrifice to maintain peace at home. It also showed the complexity of my father's position, caught between supporting me and managing my mother's volatile emotions.

These experiences undoubtedly influenced my adult relationships. I developed an unhealthy desire for older men to love me, a pattern that mirrored my childhood dynamics. My husband was 18 years older than me and a narcissist, and my last ex-boyfriend was 13 years older and also displayed narcissistic traits. The latter even called me "baby girl," a term that evoked memories of my father and made me fall for him. This pattern of seeking approval and affection from older men was a direct result of my relationship with my father and the manipulation I experienced as a child.

Growing up in an environment where my mom used triangulation to control her relationships with us, her children, left me feeling confused and emotionally scarred. Triangulation, a strategy where one person creates tension or conflict between two other people, was my mother's way of maintaining control. This often meant pitting one sibling against another, causing emotional strain and confusion. My mother's actions created an environment of distrust among us siblings, as we never knew who might be the next target. This atmosphere created a sense of competition rather than unity, making it difficult for us to form close bonds.

From a young age, I experienced intense anxiety, although, at the time, I didn't understand its source. I used to believe that my homesickness whenever I stayed overnight at a friend's or cousin's house was simply because I missed home. However, I now realize that my anxiety was deeply rooted in a trauma bond with my mother. Her behavior made me dependent on her, and being away from her caused overwhelming stress. This dependency made it hard for me to enjoy normal childhood experiences and created a sense of isolation. I often felt torn between wanting to explore the world and needing to stay close to the safety of my home.

A vivid example of triangulation in our family was how my mother would share negative thoughts about my siblings with me. She often talked about Terry's poor academic performance, labeling him as not very bright. This not only undermined Terry but also placed an unfair burden on me, as I felt compelled to succeed in avoiding similar criticism. These negative remarks made me anxious about my performance and fostered a fear of failure. It also created an unnecessary rivalry between Terry and me, which strained our relationship.

Similarly, my sister Candy was frequently the target of my mother's harsh comments. She constantly talked about how Candy was fat and lazy, how her husband drank too much, and how he was too loud and made too much work for my mom when they came to visit. It just went on and on. These conversations left me feeling distressed and conflicted. I loved my siblings and hated hearing them being disparaged. The constant negativity directed at Candy made it difficult for her to feel accepted and loved within our family. It also forced me into the role of mediator, which was emotionally exhausting.

As I grew older, I started to resist my mother's attempts to involve me in her negative narratives about my siblings. I remember a moment when I told my mom that I didn't want to hear any more negative comments about Candy. I expressed my love for Candy and my disinterest in my mother's criticisms. This confrontation was not easy, but it was necessary for my own emotional well-being and for maintaining a healthy relationship with my sister. Standing up to my mother in this way was a turning point in asserting my own boundaries. It was a small but crucial step toward breaking free from the cycle of negativity.

Despite my efforts to shield my siblings from my mother's hurtful words, there were many instances where I felt helpless. As a little girl, I would often find Candy in tears after one of my mother's hurtful remarks. I would comfort Candy, telling her that I loved her. Then, I would go to my mother and urge her to apologize and hug Candy to stop her from crying. Sometimes, my mother would listen and do as I asked, but the damage had often already been done. These moments were heartbreaking and pointed to the emotional toll my mother's behavior had on all of us. It also reinforced my role as the peacekeeper, which was an immense burden for a child.

Chapter 3: Survival Tactics-Coping with a Narcissistic Mother

From an early age, I learned a harsh truth: love wasn't something freely given; it was something you had to earn, often at a steep price. This idea of love as a transaction became the foundation of how I understood relationships, leaving scars that would take years to heal. My mother's affection was a currency I could never quite afford, always contingent upon meeting her exacting standards.

This conditional affection was often accompanied by manipulation and denial. One of the clearest examples of this from my mother involved an incident that happened when I was about four or five years old. This was back in the days when ordering from catalogs was common and packages were delivered by UPS. My mother frequently ordered items, and I vividly recall one particular instance when she invited the UPS delivery man inside for coffee. I was very young at the time, likely not even in school yet, and I remember being told to go play in my room while the delivery man sat with my mom in the kitchen. This memory stuck with me, but it wasn't until later that evening that it became significant.

That night, my mom was talking about the packages she had received. As a little kid who had seen something unusual, I innocently mentioned that she had invited the delivery man inside for coffee. My mom's reaction was immediate and intense—her face turned red with anger as she denied it ever happened. She accused me of lying, saying I didn't know what I was talking about, and insisted that the delivery man had simply dropped off the packages and left. My dad was present during this exchange, but I don't recall him saying much. What I do remember clearly is the overwhelming confusion and doubt that her reaction caused in me. I knew what I had seen, but her adamant denial made me question my own memory, which is the essence of gaslighting.

My mom was trying to make me doubt my own perception of reality by insisting that what I remembered didn't happen. She attempted to rewrite the narrative to avoid any potential repercussions, possibly out of fear that my dad would suspect something more was going on. The truth was, the UPS man did come into the house, and I was sent away so that I wouldn't witness whatever was going on. But in the moment, as a small child, I didn't understand why she would deny something so straightforward.

This pattern of manipulation extended beyond isolated incidents and was a regular part of my life. Early memories of my mother's conditional affection are deeply tied to housework. Even as a young child, I could sense the weight of her expectations. She had specific, rigid ways she wanted things done, and the pressure to meet her standards was immense. I remember the anxiety that would grip me whenever I had to clean. My stomach would twist into knots as I carefully dusted, scrubbed, and arranged everything, hoping desperately that it would be good enough for her.

But it never seemed to be. The moment she walked into the room, my heart raced, bracing for her reaction. If I hadn't met her exacting standards, which often felt impossible to achieve, she would become visibly upset. Her face would tighten, and her eyes would narrow sharply, like a magnifying glass focusing on every flaw, as she scanned the room for any imperfection. It was as if all the effort I had put in didn't matter—her disappointment would fill the space, suffocating any small sense of pride I had managed to build.

The message was painfully clear to me, even at that young age: her love and approval weren't given freely; they had to be earned, and the price was perfection. Anything less meant I had failed her; with that failure came a deep sense of shame. This planted the seeds of self-doubt and a relentless drive to meet her impossible standards that would follow me for many years.

This experience extended beyond housework into every aspect of our relationship. My mother often involved me in her conflicts with my siblings, expecting me to take her side unconditionally. She would share her negative opinions about my siblings with me, conditioning me to view them through her critical lens. If I sided with her, I was rewarded with her approval and affection. However, if I dared to disagree or show empathy toward my siblings, I was met with disapproval and a cold shoulder. This created a sense of isolation between me and my siblings, as I felt I had to distance myself from them to maintain my mother's favor. Over time, this not only affected my relationships with my siblings but also reinforced the belief that love and approval were always conditional.

My mother's conditional affection had a profound impact on my self-image, especially when it came to my appearance. She often criticized my older sister Candy for her weight, calling her "fat" and "lazy." These comments felt like warnings, showing me what would happen if I didn't meet her standards. As a result, I became fixated on staying thin, fearing that gaining weight would mean losing her approval. By the time I was 11 or 12, I had already started developing unhealthy habits to keep myself as thin as possible. I would do sit-ups obsessively in my bedroom at night—sometimes upwards of 400—believing it was the best way to keep my stomach flat and avoid her criticism. Restricting my food intake and over-exercising became ways to cope, as my self-esteem became closely tied to my appearance, driven by a desperate need for her approval.

When I entered my teenage years, these ingrained patterns became even more apparent in my relationships with others. I believed that to be loved, I had to be perfect in every way, which turned me into a people pleaser, constantly striving to meet others' expectations at the expense of my own well-being.

A significant effect of this became apparent in my marriage. My husband, like my mother, used manipulation and triangulation to control me. He would often compare me to his ex-wife, making disparaging comments about her behavior and implying that I should be different. One instance that stands out is when he mentioned that his ex-wife would "stomp around the house like an elephant." This comment made me so afraid of making any noise that I started tiptoeing around the house, terrified that if I didn't live up to his expectations, he would withdraw his love—just as my mother had done. This fear drove me to constantly try to please him, often at great personal cost.

The extent to which this behavior affected me is evident when I think back to the routines I established to gain his approval. Every morning, my husband would wake up at 6:00 a.m., and I would get up at the same time. My morning routine became centered around making sure he had a hot, home-cooked breakfast. This wasn't a simple, quick meal; I would prepare French toast, eggs, bacon—an entire feast carefully made to please him. Meanwhile, I had to manage everything else in the household. We had four pugs, each requiring attention, and I had to get my son ready for school. All of this was done before I even started my own workday. Yet, despite preparing such elaborate meals for him every morning, I rarely ate anything myself. The fear of gaining weight and losing his love was so deeply embedded in my mind, courtesy of my mother's conditioning, that I often skipped meals to maintain the image I believed he wanted.

This routine was more than just a daily habit; it was a reflection of how deeply I had internalized the belief that love required constant effort and sacrifice. I was so focused on pleasing my husband that I completely neglected my own needs. It wasn't until much later, after he became ill that I began to realize how much of my behavior had been conditioned by both him and my mother. The parallels between the two relationships were striking, and it became painfully clear that I had carried the lessons of my childhood into my adult life.

These patterns of behavior didn't develop in isolation; they had deep roots in my early experiences with my mother. When my mother took on a full-time role at my father's electrical contracting business, the dynamics at home shifted dramatically. My father had started his own business when I was around 10, initially hiring a bookkeeper to manage the office tasks. However, as the years passed, it became clear that the bookkeeper was untrustworthy, so my father ultimately let him go. Around the time I was 13 or 14, my mother stepped in to take over many of the bookkeeper's responsibilities.

One particular incident with house cleaning exemplified how her expectations were unachievable and how they affected my self-esteem. I was around 14 or 16, and my duties included cleaning the house from top to bottom. This meant moving all the furniture, dusting behind everything, and making sure that every corner of the house was spotless. I was just a teenager trying my best to meet her expectations. I felt like I was doing a good job, going above and beyond what was usually expected of someone my age. But to my mother, my efforts were never enough. The day of the incident, I had spent hours cleaning, ensuring that every part of the house was as clean as I could make it. I was exhausted but somewhat proud of my work. However, when my mother came home, her reaction shattered my sense of accomplishment. Instead of acknowledging the effort I had put in, she immediately pointed out the tiniest flaw—perhaps a speck of dust or an area that wasn't cleaned to her satisfaction. Her criticism was relentless. It didn't matter how much time or energy I had invested; all she could see was what I hadn't done perfectly. She would say things like, "It doesn't even look like you cleaned," or, "You missed this spot," as if all my hard work meant nothing.

During this period, her constant negativity and impossible standards wore me down. I began to feel like there was no point in trying because nothing I did would ever be good enough. The repeated criticism deeply affected my self-esteem. I started to believe that my efforts were worthless and that I was incapable of doing anything right. This mindset bled into other areas of my life, making me doubt my abilities and lowering my self-worth.

After the incident, I reached a breaking point. I remember lying in bed at night, crying uncontrollably. My sister, who shared a room with me, would try to console me, but I was filled with anger and despair. I hated everything about my life then—my mother, the house, the expectations placed on me. I couldn't understand why my mother couldn't just be satisfied or at least acknowledge the work I had done. The emotional burden was overwhelming, and I felt utterly defeated.

Eventually, I decided it wasn't worth it to keep trying to please her. I gave up on trying to meet her impossible standards. This wasn't an act of rebellion as much as it was a survival mechanism. I realized that whether I cleaned ideally or not, she would always find something to criticize, so I chose to stop caring about her approval. Interestingly, my mother seemed to take notice of this shift in my attitude. Instead of punishing me, she almost seemed to respect my decision. She would later tell others about how I had stood up to her, saying that I had told her, "You're going to complain whether I clean or not, so I'm just not going to do it anymore." It was as if she admired that I had finally pushed back, although I found the entire situation confusing and ironic.

This left me with a complicated understanding of effort and approval. On one hand, it taught me that there's a point where striving for someone else's approval becomes self-destructive. As the proverb goes, *"You can't pour from an empty cup,"* meaning that constantly giving to others without taking care of yourself leaves you drained and unable to continue. It highlights the idea that if you neglect your own needs in the pursuit of pleasing others, you eventually run out of the emotional and physical energy needed to function, let alone support those around you.

Another responsibility that fell to me when my mother started working was cooking dinner. No matter what I made, it never seemed to meet her standards. It was almost as if she expected me to somehow morph into her and replicate her cooking skills, even though I was just a teenager doing my best. I remember the frustration of hearing her complain about every meal I prepared simply because it wasn't exactly how she would have made it. Despite this, I didn't stop cooking—after all, we all had to eat. But it was disheartening to know my efforts would always be compared to hers and found lacking.

There was one silver lining, though—my dad. He never made a fuss about the food. In fact, he would quietly thank me for dinner and tell me he thought it was good. His appreciation, even if it was understated, meant the world to me. In contrast to my mother's relentless criticism, his simple acknowledgment felt like a breath of fresh air. It's funny to think how that small gesture shaped my future relationships.

My husband, for instance, always expected me to cook, but the difference was that he appreciated it. Even if the meal didn't turn out perfectly, he would still say thank you and maybe even eat it with a smile. I often wonder if he genuinely liked everything I made, but the simple act of showing gratitude made all the difference. Looking back, I can see how low my expectations for love had become. This small gesture of appreciation—one of the few things he ever praised me for—kept me in the relationship for years. When you're used to receiving nothing but criticism or indifference, even the tiniest breadcrumb of kindness feels like a whole loaf of bread.

Over time, I've come to realize that I'm actually a pretty stellar cook. Friends who've joined me for Thanksgiving or who've tasted my dishes often rave about my cooking. It's ironic that something my mother criticized so much became a skill I genuinely enjoy and excel at. But here's the catch—I only enjoy cooking when I don't feel forced to do it. When it becomes an obligation, all the joy drains out of it, and I'm reminded of those early years when nothing I did seemed good enough.

It's funny, in a way—who knew that dusting and cooking could become life lessons in conditional love? It took a long time, and more than a few missed dust bunnies, to unlearn the lessons my mother had instilled in me about approval and self-worth.

Throughout my life, I've relied on two main coping strategies to manage stress and emotional challenges. The first is throwing myself into tasks—finding things to do, staying busy, and diving headfirst into projects. The second, which has been a struggle for much of my life, is dealing with an eating disorder. Both of these strategies have been my way of trying to maintain some control when life feels overwhelming.

When things get tough, my instinct is to stay busy—really busy. If there's a task to be done, you can bet I'm all over it. I've always found that keeping myself occupied helps me avoid dealing with difficult emotions. It's like I'm playing a game of emotional hide-and-seek, except I'm hiding from myself and hoping I never get found. The logic is simple: if I'm busy enough, I won't have the time or energy to think about what's really bothering me. Of course, this approach often backfires. I end up like a circus performer trying to juggle too many plates—eventually, they all come crashing down. Instead of addressing the root of the problem, I just pile on more tasks, thinking that if I can keep everything in order, I'll magically feel better. Spoiler alert: it doesn't work that way.

This coping mechanism hit a roadblock earlier this year. In February, I had an accident while trying to get on my horse. I fell and broke my ribs, leaving me physically unable to do much of anything. Suddenly, my go-to strategy for coping—staying busy—was off the table. I couldn't clean, couldn't run errands, couldn't do any of the things I usually turned to when life got overwhelming. My son had to step in to help me around the house because I couldn't even lift things. This was incredibly frustrating and left me feeling helpless and depressed. Without the ability to stay busy, I was forced to confront my emotions head-on, and it was tough. I realized then how much I had been relying on staying busy as a way to avoid dealing with my feelings.

The other coping mechanism that has been a constant in my life is my struggle with an eating disorder. This began as a way to gain control in situations where I felt powerless. Food became something I could control, and it spiraled into unhealthy habits that have been hard to break. Even though I'm aware of how destructive this behavior is, it's been challenging to let go of, especially during times of stress.

Reflecting on these coping mechanisms, I can see how they both stem from a need to feel in control when my emotions are overwhelming. Unfortunately, neither strategy is healthy or effective in the long term. Staying busy until

I'm exhausted or turning to an eating disorder only masks the underlying issues rather than addressing them. I've come to understand that my inability to develop healthier coping mechanisms has deep roots in my childhood and my relationship with my mother.

My mother played a role in shaping these coping strategies. As mentioned, from a young age, I felt the need to please her, meet her impossible standards, and gain her approval. Even after I got married, this dynamic didn't change. My mother would call me during work hours, expecting me to drop everything to listen to her complaints or to take her side in arguments with my father. It didn't matter that I was busy at work; she assumed that it was okay to disrupt my day because I was dating my boss. This placed me in a difficult position where I felt torn between my responsibilities at work and my need to be there for my mother. My boss, later my husband, didn't make things easier. He would walk by my office door, giving me disapproving looks if I stayed on the phone too long. It was a constant battle between wanting to meet my mother's demands and maintaining my professional responsibilities. This experience reinforced my belief that I had to keep everyone happy, often at my expense.

Art has been one of the few outlets where I can express my emotions, although even this has been shaped by my struggles, like a canvas that absorbs every brushstroke of pain and sadness. For many years, I painted sad-faced girls. These paintings directly reflected how I felt inside—sad, overwhelmed, and unable to express my feelings in any other way. The girls in my paintings always ended up with tears, no matter how they started. This artistic expression was my way of coping with emotions I didn't know how to handle. However, it also became a reflection of my inability to move beyond those feelings. People often asked me why I didn't paint something happy, and I didn't have an answer. I just knew this was how I felt, and this was what came out when I put brush to canvas.

In terms of relationships, my coping strategies have made it difficult to form and maintain healthy connections with others. Despite this, two close friendships have stood the test of time. One of these friendships goes back more than 20 years. Although I haven't always been my best friend, this person has always been there for me, even when I didn't deserve it. She's like an angel in my life, and her unwavering support has meant more to me than I can express.

My other close friendship is with a woman I've known for about six or seven years. Our lives are remarkably similar, and we've been able to support each other through some tough times. She's much younger than me, but she's going through many of the same challenges I faced at her age. I admire her ability to recognize and confront these issues earlier in life than I did. While I'm still learning to cope in healthier ways, seeing her journey has given me hope that it's possible.

Romantic relationships have been another area where my coping strategies have impacted my life. My first marriage was short-lived, and I've often wondered if I left because my husband wasn't a narcissist, and I found that too boring. After that, I was drawn to narcissistic partners, likely because it mirrored the dynamic I had with my mother. My second husband, who recently passed away, was also a narcissist. These relationships were filled with the same patterns of trying to please, trying to be good enough, and constantly feeling like I was falling short. It's only now, after years of reflection, that I realize how these patterns have played out in my relationships and how much they've been influenced by my early experiences with my mother.

I'm still working on developing healthier coping mechanisms. It's a struggle, but I'm learning that it's okay to slow down, not have everything perfectly under control, and express my emotions in ways that don't involve staying busy or falling back into disordered eating. As Rumi once wrote, *"The wound is the place where the Light enters you."* It's a process, and I'm far from perfect at it, but I'm starting to understand that real coping involves facing my emotions head-on rather than trying to outrun them.

Chapter 4: The Invisible Scars of Emotional Abuse

Anxiety has been a constant shadow in my life, but for years, I never fully understood where it came from. I grew up in a household filled with tension and unpredictability, where my parents' constant fighting created a storm of chaos. Naturally, I believed this turmoil was the root of my anxiety. It wasn't until recently, however, that I uncovered a deeper, more insidious cause—narcissistic abuse. This type of abuse is like an invisible poison, slowly seeping into the soul and manifesting in ways that are hard to see but deeply damaging, much like hidden roots that quietly undermine the foundation of even the strongest trees.

It took me years to connect the dots between my anxiety and the emotional scars left by growing up in a narcissistic household. Narcissistic abuse is often subtle, making it difficult to recognize, especially when compared to the more overt forms of abuse like physical or verbal assaults. I didn't realize that the constant need for approval, the feeling of never being enough, and the low self-esteem that plagued me into adulthood were all products of this abuse. It became clear that these entrenched insecurities were not just personality quirks but symptoms of a long-term emotional wound.

As I entered adulthood, these issues didn't simply disappear; they evolved and manifested in my relationships. I found myself repeatedly drawn to narcissistic partners without even realizing it. My son's biological father, my husband, and even a recent partner all exhibited narcissistic traits. At the time, I didn't understand why I kept attracting these people. It felt like a curse; as if I was destined to be in unhealthy, toxic relationships. Each failed relationship reinforced my belief that I was unworthy of love, trapping me in a cycle of self-doubt and despair.

It wasn't until this year that I started to dig deeper into my past and confront these patterns. Through inner child work and self-reflection, I began to recognize the underlying issues driving my choices. The low self-esteem I had carried for so long was a major factor. I had been conditioned to believe that I wasn't worthy of a healthy relationship, that chaos and dysfunction were normal, even desirable. It was a mix of grief and relief—grief for the years lost to this damaging mindset and relief that I could now begin to change it.

This realization hit me hard. I had always thought that if a relationship didn't feel chaotic, it wasn't real or meaningful. The chaos had become a twisted form of comfort, something familiar that I subconsciously sought out. This belief system, deeply ingrained in my childhood, had led me to mistake drama for love and stability for boredom. It was a painful truth to accept, but necessary for my growth. Learning to value peace and stability in relationships has been an enlightening experience, reshaping my understanding of what true love should feel like.

My relationship with my son's biological father began a troubling pattern. We met in college, and I ended up getting pregnant. Although we weren't married, we were tied together by our son. It was during a court battle over visitation rights that he was diagnosed with narcissistic personality disorder. The psychologist met with each of us individually, and while the diagnosis explained much of his behavior, it didn't resonate with me at the time. I was young and more focused on ensuring he wouldn't get visitation rights than on understanding the implications of the diagnosis. The term "narcissist" didn't hold much meaning for me back then; all I cared about was protecting my son and moving forward without having to worry about his father's involvement.

When my son was three, I married my first husband, Brian. In hindsight, he was probably the only non-narcissistic partner I've ever had. However, I ended up leaving him for a narcissistic partner, Dan who would later become my second husband. Dan had dementia and after having to place him in a home this led me to a period of deep reflection, revealing how I was often drawn to the very things that were detrimental to my well-being. Dan passed away from dementia in 2024.

The trauma bond that develops in these types of relationships is powerful. When a parent is a narcissist, you grow accustomed to receiving love in unpredictable, conditional doses. This creates a cycle where you're constantly seeking approval, always hoping that the love will be consistent and unconditional this time. But it never is. Instead, the love is given and then cruelly withheld, creating a bond that is hard to break. This cycle leaves deep emotional scars, making it difficult to trust and love healthily. We start asking ourselves questions like: Why is it so hard to break free from this cycle? Why do I continue to seek approval that was never truly given?

As I began to understand these dynamics, I realized that my relationships were not about love at all—they were about control and familiarity. The anxiety that had plagued me for so long was not just a reaction to external stressors; it was deeply tied to the emotional manipulation and conditional love I had experienced growing up. *The Emotionally Absent Mother* by Jasmin Lee Cori explores how early emotional neglect can lead to lifelong patterns of anxiety and unhealthy relationships, highlighting the deep connections between past trauma and present-day struggles. Cori examines the subtle yet impactful effects of growing up without emotional support, showing how these early wounds can shape one's sense of self and influence the relationships one seeks in adulthood.

Reflecting on my own experiences, I can see how growing up under the control of my narcissistic mother affected my ability to form and maintain friendships. My mother manipulated us to prevent building relationships outside of our family, creating an environment where social interactions were rare and often discouraged. Anytime I had a friend over in elementary school, she would criticize and point out everything she didn't like about that friend after they left. This was a form of triangulation and manipulation designed to keep me under her control and prevent me from forming meaningful connections with others. This isolation left me shy and unsure of myself in social situations, as I lacked the opportunity to develop the skills necessary to build meaningful connections with peers.

One of the few opportunities I had to socialize was during visits to my aunt and uncle's home, about 45 minutes away. My aunt, a kind and caring woman, often invited me to stay for a week during the summer to play with my cousin my age. These visits were a rare chance for me to interact with someone my age, but despite my excitement, I could never stay the full week. Each time, as night approached, I would be overwhelmed with anxiety—a deep, almost crippling attachment to my mother that I didn't fully understand at the time. The moment nighttime came, I would cry and insist on calling home, unable to bear the separation. My aunt, understanding and patient, would always drive me back the next day, recognizing that my "homesickness" was more about the trauma bond I had with my mother than any true longing for home.

This experience wasn't confined to my aunt's house. The anxiety of being away from my mother made it nearly impossible for me to enjoy normal childhood experiences, let alone form lasting friendships. Even in familiar and welcoming environments like my cousin's home, the pull to return to my mother was stronger than my desire to socialize.

As the saying goes, *"Home is where the heart is,"* but for me, home was where the anxiety lived, deeply rooted in my connection to my mother. This anxiety interfered with my ability to connect with others, making it difficult to build and maintain relationships outside of my family.

From kindergarten through fourth grade, school was an emotional battlefield for me. Each day, as I was forced to spend hours away from my mother, I felt an overwhelming sense of despair that I couldn't fully understand at the time. I would retreat to the bathroom to cry, overwhelmed by a feeling I described as "homesickness," though it was much more complex than that. When looking back, I now realize that it was a manifestation of trauma bonding—a deep emotional dependency on my mother that made any separation feel like a form of psychological torture.

This emotional turmoil made it nearly impossible for me to engage in school activities like a normal child. While my classmates were adjusting to the routine of being away from home all day, I struggled to make it through even a few hours without feeling an intense need to return to my mother. The idea of spending an entire day at school, surrounded by peers who seemed so comfortable and at ease, was something I couldn't comprehend. The emotional pain of being apart from my mother overshadowed everything else, making it difficult to focus on learning, making friends, or enjoying the typical childhood experiences that others seemed to embrace so easily.

My struggles were compounded by the fact that I never felt like I could be part of the social world that my peers inhabited. While I remained on the sidelines, they would talk about sleepovers, playing at each other's houses, and their adventures with friends. Even when I was invited to join in, I couldn't bring myself to go. The thought of being away from my mother, even for a few hours in a fun setting, was too overwhelming. Knowing that my mother would likely say no, I would shy away from invitations, reinforcing my isolation. Over time, this created a barrier between me and my peers, making it even harder to develop the social skills that were so crucial during those formative years.

As a result, I grew up feeling isolated and disconnected from the world around me. This sense of isolation followed me into adulthood, where I continued to grapple with the effects of that early trauma bond. On the surface, I may seem outgoing and eager to socialize, but the reality is that I find it incredibly difficult to be around people for extended periods. I can handle social situations for a short time, but I quickly become overwhelmed and feel the need to retreat. The anxiety and discomfort that stem from those early experiences still linger, influencing my ability to engage fully with the world.

Despite these challenges, I'm grateful that I haven't passed this anxiety onto my son. Unlike me, he is comfortable facing the world on his own, able to go out and do things without the crippling fear that once held me back. While he, like most people, enjoys having company, he doesn't rely on it the way I did—and still do. I see him confidently exploring the world in ways I never could, and it gives me hope. Though I still limit myself to a few familiar places where I feel safe, such as certain restaurants or cafes, I'm slowly learning to push past my comfort zone. It's a small step but an important one as I continue to work on breaking free from the shadows of my past.

Lately, I've been thinking a lot about narcissism, especially because it's becoming a more widely recognized issue. Back in the 1990s, Sam Vaknin was one of the first to really bring the term "narcissist" into the public conversation, but at the time, it wasn't something people talked about much. When my son's biological father was labeled a narcissist, I didn't give it much thought. I was relieved because I knew someone like that wouldn't be a healthy influence in my son's life. So, I moved on without fully grasping the significance of that label. It wasn't until recent years, as narcissism has become more openly discussed, that I started to understand the depth and impact of narcissistic abuse.

This growing awareness of narcissism has made me reflect on why I've been considering calling my book *"The Silent Abuse."* Narcissistic abuse is insidious because it's not something people easily see. It's often kept hidden, not just from others but even from ourselves. The manipulation is so subtle and pervasive that, like the metaphorical slow boil, you don't realize it's happening until you're already deeply affected. When you do start to speak out, it's easy for others to dismiss your experiences as exaggerated or even irrational. This is especially true when dealing with a covert narcissist like my husband, Dan, who could charm everyone around him. To the outside world, he was charismatic and likable, so if I had ever spoken up about his abusive behavior, people would have thought I was crazy.

The most challenging aspect of dealing with narcissists is the way they present themselves to the world. Dan was a master at portraying himself as the ideal husband and father. He was charming, sociable, and could easily win people over. Meanwhile, I was living a completely different reality, one filled with emotional manipulation and control. Not only would people not have believed me, but Dan had also gaslit, twisted, and manipulated my own reality so much that I didn't even believe the truth of the situation myself or realize what was happening to me. As the saying goes, "*If you repeat a lie often enough, it becomes accepted as truth,*" and Dan had mastered this tactic to the point where even I questioned my own perceptions. The public persona he maintained was so convincing that it would have been my word against his, and in the court of public opinion, he would have won every time. This is one of the reasons why narcissistic abuse is so isolating—it's hard to make people understand what they don't see.

This isolation is precisely why it's so important for survivors to speak out. The more we share our stories and bring the truth to light, the more we can help others who are going through similar experiences. It's crucial to convey to readers that narcissistic abuse is real, even if it's not visible to the outside world. The more we use our voices, the more we can validate each other's experiences. When we tell our stories, we not only heal ourselves but also help others feel seen and heard. It's through this collective sharing of truth that we can begin to dismantle the myths and misconceptions about narcissistic abuse.

The path to recognizing and coming to terms with narcissistic abuse is challenging yet crucial. As Maya Angelou once said, *"There is no greater agony than bearing an untold story inside you."* By coming forward and telling our stories, we shine a light on a form of abuse that thrives in the shadows. It's not easy to speak out, especially when the world sees the abuser so differently from how we experience them. But by doing so, we can start to change the narrative. We can help others recognize the signs, trust their own experiences, and, ultimately, find the strength to break free from the cycle of abuse. The more we speak, the more we empower ourselves and others to stand up against this silent, insidious form of abuse.

Chapter 5: Stepping into Adulthood-The Search for Love

"Independence is the first step toward self-discovery."

That's what I told myself as I arrived at college, a place that felt like a gateway to the freedom I had longed for. My entire life, I had been under strict supervision, with little to no freedom. College was my first real taste of independence, and I embraced it wholeheartedly, eager to explore everything it had to offer. The excitement was overwhelming, and I was determined to make the most of it. I quickly made friends with a few girls in my dorm, which was an all-girls dorm in a Catholic college. We bonded over our shared excitement for the freedom we were experiencing and soon found ourselves diving headfirst into the college party scene, with every night bringing a new adventure.

Every night, we would find ourselves at some party or another, whether it was a casual gathering in someone's room or a full-blown event at a club. The dorms were co-ed, but the floors were separated by gender. I lived on the fifth floor, the top floor, and directly below us were the boys. On the second floor, some guys had a knack for doctoring I.D.s, allowing us to get into 21+ clubs without a problem. My friends and I took full advantage of this, spending countless nights dancing and meeting new people, including upperclassmen who seemed much older and cooler then.

Despite the wild nights, I managed to keep up with my classes, though my social life was my top priority. The thrill of independence was intoxicating, and I wanted to experience everything college offered. I met the man who would become my son's biological father during this time. He lived off-campus, which I found incredibly appealing and mature. At the time, I didn't realize he had been kicked off campus; all I saw was the allure of his independence and the company of upperclassmen. He was a sophomore, a year older than me, and lived with other juniors and seniors who threw frequent parties. These parties were filled with dancing and music, creating an atmosphere far from the strict environment I had known growing up. It was easy to get swept up in the excitement of it all, and before I knew it, I was spending more time at his place than in my own dorm.

He was Dominican and had a certain charm that I found irresistible. To me, he was captivating, and he knew exactly what to say to make me feel special and noticed. His smooth talk and confident demeanor were like nothing I had ever encountered before. Looking back, I realize that he displayed many traits common to narcissistic men. He was obsessed with his appearance and knew how to present himself in a way that was both alluring and manipulative. At that time in my life, I was starved for love and attention, so when he showered me with both, I was drawn to him like a moth to a flame. It was as if he had tapped into a deep longing within me, one that I wasn't even fully aware of, and used it to pull me closer and closer.

Earlier in the year, I had briefly dated another guy from the basketball team. He was nice enough, but we didn't have much of a connection, and the relationship fizzled out quickly. It was a different story when I met my son's biological father. He seemed completely captivated by me, a behavior I now recognize as a common tactic used by narcissists to draw their victims in. Having grown up with little affection, I was desperate for the kind of attention he was giving me. It was as though I had been wandering in a desert, parched and thirsty, and he came along with a bucket of water. I couldn't get enough. I was blinded by his charm, mistaking his intense interest for genuine love and care when it was much darker in reality.

The thrill of a budding romance quickly faded when I discovered I was pregnant during my second year of college. At that point, my boyfriend and I had moved off campus together, which initially felt like a natural progression of our relationship. However, it quickly became clear that the move began a dark chapter. As soon as I got pregnant, he began to change, revealing a side of himself that I hadn't seen before. He started going out alone more frequently, often disappearing for days at a time without any explanation. Cell phones weren't common back then, so there was no way to reach him, leaving me alone and worried, wondering where he was and what he was doing.

I graduated high school in 1991, which was around 1991 or 1992, and my son was born in 1993. As the months went by, his behavior became increasingly erratic. He began showing signs of drug use, something I had never known about or experienced before. The man I thought I knew seemed to vanish, replaced by someone distant, unreliable, and often high. This drastic shift left me feeling isolated and scared, especially as I tried to manage my pregnancy. Our life together, which had once felt like an exciting adventure, quickly spiraled into something unrecognizable. I was a college student trying to balance school, work, and the overwhelming responsibilities of impending motherhood, all while dealing with a partner who was becoming more of a stranger every day.

Eventually, I couldn't keep up with the rent on our apartment. He refused to work, leaving me to try and make ends meet with a part-time job while attending classes full-time. It was impossible, and I knew I couldn't continue living that way. With no other options, I made the difficult decision to move back home. At that point, I was nearly six months pregnant, but I was so tiny from not eating properly that it was easy to hide. I wore baggy shirts, and no one could tell that I was expecting. I was terrified to tell my parents, convinced that they would react with anger or disappointment, especially my father, whom I had always feared. The anxiety of keeping my pregnancy a secret was crushing, and I dreaded the moment when I would have to reveal the truth.

When I finally worked up the courage to tell my mom, I begged her not to tell my dad. I was convinced that his reaction would be explosive, and I couldn't bear the thought of facing his anger. To my surprise, my mom agreed to keep it between us, but the stress of the situation didn't lessen. Elias's biological father got me a bus ticket, and I left. I moved to New York City that night while my parents were still at work. The decision to leave was driven by fear and desperation. He had pressured me to have an abortion, but by then, I was nearly six months pregnant, and I could feel the baby moving inside me. I couldn't go through with it, and I knew I had to leave.

We ended up staying at his mother's house, but his behavior didn't change. He continued going out every night, coming home drunk or high, if he came home at all. I was naive, having grown up in an environment where I had little exposure to drugs or alcohol. The extent of my experimentation had been a few drinks with friends after high school graduation. The world he was involved in was foreign and frightening to me. I had no idea how to deal with his addiction or the erratic behavior that came with it. My life felt like it was spiraling out of control, and I didn't know how to stop it.

When my son was born, the situation only got worse. He would leave for days at a time, leaving me alone with a newborn, with no idea where he was or when he would return. Without cell phones, I had no way of reaching him, and I was left in the dark, wondering if he was even alive. We had no money; he wasn't working, and I had to rely on government assistance just to provide for my baby. I received W.I.C. (Women, Infants, and Children) benefits, which helped with formula, but it wasn't enough. I also received welfare, but the small amount barely covered the cost of diapers and wipes. I was constantly stressed, trying to figure out how to make ends meet while caring for a newborn on my own.

The few times he was home, he didn't contribute anything to our household. He wasn't bringing in any money, and what little we had was quickly used up on basic necessities. At one point, he revealed his deep-seated racism, admitting he was with me because he hated white people and wanted to use me. It was a shocking and hurtful revelation that added to the turmoil of our already chaotic life. I felt completely abandoned, both emotionally and financially, as I struggled to provide for my son. The reality of being a young, single mother hit me hard, and I realized that the man I had once loved was not going to be the partner or father I had hoped for. The dream of building a life together had shattered, leaving me to pick up the pieces and figure out how to move forward independently.

With the weight of those harsh realities bearing down on me, living in New York City in the early nineties only intensified my challenges. The city had a raw, gritty energy, and I was thrust into a overwhelming and unforgiving world. One of the harsh realities I quickly learned was that survival often required resourcefulness and a willingness to do things that, under normal circumstances, you wouldn't even consider. For example, there were these small bodegas scattered around the city—many of them fronts for drug operations. They were places where people would exchange food stamps for cash, usually at a steep loss. Most of the people doing this were buying drugs, and the dealers knew it. However, I was in a different situation. There was a bodega just a block from where I lived, and the people there quickly realized that I wasn't trading my food stamps for drugs. I was selling them because I needed cash to buy diapers, wipes, and other essentials for my baby.

Normally, they would only give you fifty cents on the dollar, but they saw that I was desperate and trying to care for my child, so they gave me an even exchange, dollar for dollar. It was a small gesture of kindness in a city that wasn't known for its compassion. I didn't know what I was doing initially; I just had to provide for my son. I asked around and talked to a few people who told me about these bodegas, and I did what I had to do. It was a tough, demeaning process, but when you're a young mother with no one to help you, pride takes a backseat to survival.

As time passed, the man I had once loved became more and more abusive. It wasn't just the emotional neglect or the endless nights he spent away from home, high and God knows where. It was physical. He would come home, often in the middle of the night, intoxicated or high, and he would force himself on me. Our son, Elias, would be sleeping in the same room, just a few feet away. I would plead with him to leave me alone, to stop, but it didn't matter. He would cover my mouth and do what he wanted, leaving me feeling powerless and violated. The reality of my situation was horrifying, but I felt trapped.

I was terrified of getting pregnant again, so six weeks after Elias was born, I got a Depo-Provera shot, which is a form of birth control. I didn't tell him, of course. I just knew that I couldn't go through another pregnancy, not in the situation I was in. The abuse continued, and it got to the point where I was living in constant fear. The turning point came one night during a particularly violent argument. Narcissists are known for their explosive tempers, and that night, his rage escalated to a terrifying level. I don't even remember what we were arguing about, but suddenly, he had me pinned against the wall. His hands were around my throat, squeezing so hard that I couldn't breathe. I was suffocating, and I honestly thought I was going to die right there in that tiny apartment.

What saved me was the sound of Elias crying. He was just a baby, lying on the bed a few feet away, and his cries broke through the madness of the moment. His cousin, who was home then, heard Elias and came into the room to see what was happening. When he saw what was happening, he pulled Elias's father off me. I was left gasping for air, my neck bruised and sore, and it was clear that I couldn't stay there any longer. The next day, I called my parents. I was too ashamed and afraid to tell them the whole truth, but I think my dad could hear the desperation in my voice.

He didn't ask too many questions; he just asked if I wanted to come home. When I said yes, he told me he would get me a bus ticket and that I should pack my things and be ready to leave the next morning. He must have known something was seriously wrong, but he didn't push me for details, which was a relief. I just needed to get out of there, and I didn't have the strength to explain everything over the phone. He was the one who got me home when I didn't have any money and no way to escape the nightmare I was living in. The bus ride back to my parents' house was a blur. I was exhausted, physically and emotionally drained, but I knew I was making the right decision.

At that time, when Elias's biological father and I were living together, our situation had become truly desperate. We couldn't afford basic necessities, so we didn't have phone service or any real means of communication. My dad, who worked in the city a lot, didn't even know where I lived, but he would drive around the area looking for me. He'd often find me and notice how skinny I was from not eating properly. He'd always offer me money, usually $20 or $50, insisting that I take it to buy food and necessities.

My dad would tell me, "You're getting so skinny. You're not eating. Why don't you just come home?" I was scared to tell him I was pregnant, fearing his reaction. He'd reassure me, saying, "I won't tell your mother I saw you because she'll make you come home whether you like it or not." Despite the difficult circumstances, my dad tried to be supportive and help me as much as possible without pushing me too hard.

My upbringing played a major role in my vulnerability to narcissistic abuse in my romantic relationships. Growing up, I lacked the emotional support and love children typically receive from their parents. This deprivation created a deep longing within me—a need to be loved, valued, and noticed. Narcissists are skilled at identifying and exploiting such vulnerabilities. They use a tactic called "love bombing," where they shower you with attention, affection, and praise, making you feel like you've finally found the love you've been missing. This is how they mirror your desires and hook you into the relationship. In my case, I was primed to fall for this tactic because I was so desperate for the affection I had been denied throughout my life.

One book that thoroughly examines the dynamics of narcissistic relationships and how individuals become vulnerable to them is *"The Human Magnet Syndrome: The Codependent Narcissist Trap"* by Ross Rosenberg. This book explores the psychology behind why certain people are drawn to narcissists, much like magnets, due to unresolved emotional needs from their upbringing. Rosenberg discusses the concept of "codependency" and how childhood experiences, much like mine, set the stage for these unhealthy relationships. The book provides insights into how narcissists use love bombing and other manipulative tactics to create an emotional bond with their victims, making it difficult to break free.

At the time, my relationship style was likely codependent, coupled with an anxious attachment. This combination made me particularly susceptible to the manipulations of a narcissist. Codependent individuals often seek validation and approval from others, while those with an anxious attachment style tend to fear abandonment and crave closeness. Narcissists exploit these traits. Although I don't remember all the details, I'm sure that I was trauma-bonded to Elias's biological father. Narcissists often create this bond by alternating between intense affection and cruel devaluation, leaving you constantly chasing the high of their approval.

One of the most insidious aspects of narcissistic relationships is that even after they end, the narcissist often tries to maintain control over you. Many narcissists, especially those like Elias's biological father, continue to pursue their victims long after the relationship is over. They use tactics like showing up unexpectedly or using your children as a way to re-enter your life. For example, on my son's 29th birthday, his father showed up at my son's house, sitting outside first thing in the morning, waiting for him. Narcissists often use children to get to the parent, exploiting their role as the other parent to keep a connection to you, even when you've made it clear that you want nothing to do with them.

After enduring such a traumatic experience, I became wary of men who reminded me of him in any way. Unfortunately, I initially misidentified the cause of the abuse, attributing it to his race rather than his narcissistic personality. This led me to make misguided decisions in my future relationships, thinking that choosing someone of a different race would protect me from similar abuse. For instance, when I met my second husband, Dan, I believed that he would be a safe choice because he was a businessman and presented himself as professional and put-together. I thought that by choosing someone who appeared stable and came from a different background, I was picking wisely. However, I failed to recognize that the core issue wasn't race but the narcissistic behavior patterns that I was drawn to due to my unresolved trauma.

The impact of the abuse cycle didn't stop there. The love bombing phase of the relationship felt so euphoric that I found myself constantly seeking that same feeling in future relationships. When someone new would show me intense interest and make me feel like the center of their world, I would be immediately drawn in, not realizing that this could be another narcissist starting the cycle all over again. This pattern of attraction and subsequent devaluation became a recurring theme, leaving me feeling more disillusioned and hurt each time.

Narcissists have a way of making you feel like you're on top of the world, only to pull the rug out from under you once they've secured your attachment. They start to devalue you, making you question your worth and feel like you're never good enough. This intermittent reinforcement—alternating between affection and rejection—keeps you hooked, hoping that if you can just do better or be better, you will return to the loving person you thought you were. It's a cruel game, and by the time you realize what's happening, the damage is often already done.

As Ross Rosenberg puts it, *"Narcissists are like emotional vampires, sucking the life out of you until there's nothing left."* By the time you recognize their true nature, it's like waking up to find that the ground beneath you has eroded away, leaving you teetering on the edge, having already lost so much of yourself.

Chapter 6: Motherhood and Manipulation-Co-Parenting with a Narcissist

How do you find your footing as a mother when you're still figuring out who you are? At 20, I was thrust into motherhood, a responsibility that demanded more of me than I could have imagined. The transition wasn't just challenging; it was life-altering. When Elias was almost five months old, I was back at my parents' house—not because I wanted to, but because I needed to. It was a place that offered some stability but also reintroduced old struggles, particularly with my mother, whose need to control my life only intensified once I returned.

I stayed home with Elias until he was about a year old, devoting all my time and energy to caring for him. My life was centered entirely around him, as I had little in common with people my age who were still in college or starting their careers. I watched from a distance as my peers lived lives of freedom and exploration while mine revolved around diapers and midnight feedings. I had no social life or personal freedom, but Elias was my world, and I poured every ounce of love into being the best mother I could be. Even in the quiet, lonely moments when I felt the weight of isolation pressing down on me, I knew my sacrifices were for him. My dreams and desires took a backseat because nothing mattered more to me than ensuring he had everything he needed.

When Elias turned one, I started working as a secretary at my parents' company. The job was necessary to provide for my son, but it was far from easy. I earned a modest wage of $6 an hour, and more than half of my income went toward daycare expenses. My daily routine was exhausting: waking up early, taking Elias to daycare, working all day, and then picking him up in the evening. My days were long and tiring, with little time for anything other than work and caring for my son.

Financially, it was a struggle. My mother, ever controlling, made sure that I never had enough money to move out and live independently. She wanted to keep me under her influence, and she did so by ensuring that I remained financially dependent. Despite living at home, I was responsible for covering all of Elias's expenses, from baby food to clothing. I scrimped and saved every penny, but it was never enough to gain the independence I longed for. I often found myself lying awake at night, wondering, *Will I ever be able to break free? How much longer can I endure this?* The weight of financial insecurity and my mother's control left me questioning whether I would ever have the chance to build a life of my own, a life where I could make decisions for myself and my son without interference.

When Elias was a year and a half old, I met Brian, who would become my first husband. Our relationship developed quickly, and we were married when Elias was three. While

Brian provided some stability, our marriage brought its own set of challenges, especially due to the ongoing issues with Elias's biological father, Fern. Fern's presence in our lives was disruptive and inconsistent. He didn't pay child support regularly and often dragged me to court over custody issues, only to fail to show up on the scheduled court dates. This repeated pattern of legal battles without resolution was frustrating and draining.

Fern's behavior was a constant source of stress, and it wasn't until Elias was around 12 or 13 that the situation began to make more sense. During our last court battle, the court required us to see a psychologist due to the ongoing custody issues. It was then that Fern was diagnosed with narcissistic personality disorder. The diagnosis explained much of his manipulative and erratic behavior, but it didn't bring any real resolution. Instead, it highlighted the psychological turmoil he had caused over the years.

The final court hearing for my son Elias's biological father, Fern, was the only one he ever attended. This was significant because he decided to show up this time despite his consistent absence and failure to meet his responsibilities. However, his attendance did not result in any visitation rights being granted. The court saw through the situation, recognizing the deeper issues at play, and denied him access. This ended a long, stressful period of legal battles and uncertainty.

When all of this began, I was married to my first husband, Brian. Elias was around five years old at the time. It was during this period that I started working for Dan, who would later become my second husband. That's how we met and eventually got together, leading to my divorce from Brian. The legal battles with Fern didn't end with my first marriage; they continued as I transitioned into a new chapter of my life with Dan.

Dan was with me through most of the court proceedings. He was a tall, imposing figure, and his presence alone was enough to intimidate. I vividly remember one particular court appearance when Fern walked by us. Dan wasn't yet my husband, but he was protective of me in a way that made me feel secure despite his own flaws. As Fern passed, Dan stood up and positioned himself almost like a shield between us, staring Fern down with a look that spoke volumes. It was as if he was silently warning Fern to back off. It was in moments like these that Dan's protective nature came through, even though, deep down, I knew he had his own set of issues.

Dan once commented that Fern's actions had nothing to do with wanting to see Elias; he just wanted to get back at me. Dan was right. Fern's behavior was never about being a father to Elias. It was about control and revenge. Narcissists often act out of a desire to maintain power over others, and Fern was no different. His court filings and attempts to gain visitation were more about manipulating me than about caring for our son. It was as if every move he made was designed to keep me on edge, to remind me that he still had the ability to disrupt my life. The entire process felt like a game to him, one where the stakes were my peace of mind and Elias's stability.

Throughout all of this, I worked hard to shield Elias from the chaos. He was too young to understand what was happening, and I didn't want to burden him with the details. While I dealt with the stress of court battles, I made sure that Elias's life remained as normal as possible. I didn't discuss the situation with him unless it was absolutely necessary. Even when he was older, around 12 or 13, and had to participate in the court process, I did my best to protect him from the full extent of the turmoil.

My relationship with Elias has always been close, perhaps too close at times. From the beginning, it was just the two of us against the world. I felt an overwhelming need to protect him from everything, even from life itself. This protective instinct was so strong that it often bordered on overprotection. Elias would sometimes tell me as a teenager, "Just let me live, Mom." But I couldn't help it. My experiences with Fern and the constant battles we faced made me feel that I needed to shield Elias from any possible harm.

Despite the challenges, our bond has remained strong. We've had our ups and downs, as all relationships do, but we've always found a way to work through them. The difficult times have brought us closer, and we've learned to face life together, supporting each other along the way. *"Adversity doesn't build character; it reveals it,"* and in our case, it revealed the depth of our connection. Through every trial, I've realized that our bond is unbreakable, forged in the fires of hardship, and strengthened by our firm commitment. In the moments when life seemed too heavy to bear, our shared resilience carried us through, reminding me that we were never truly alone.

One of the most challenging moments in our relationship occurred when Elias was around five years old. Elias, being of mixed heritage with Dominican roots from Fern's side, has a darker complexion than Brian and me, who were blonde and blue-eyed. One day, Elias asked me, "How come I have brown skin and yours is peach?" It was a question that caught me off guard, but I knew I had to answer him truthfully, even if he was only five years old.

I gently explained to him that Brian was not his biological father. I told him that he had another father who lived far away and that this father was the reason for his darker skin. I kept the explanation simple, not wanting to overwhelm him with details he was too young to understand. At that moment, I realized the complexity of our situation, like trying to untangle a knot with many hidden strands, but I also knew that honesty was the best approach, even if it meant confronting difficult truths.

"The struggle you're in today is developing the strength you need for tomorrow." This quote connects deeply with my experience of raising Elias. The years of legal battles and the challenges of raising him in such a challenging environment were indeed struggles that tested us both. Each obstacle, each moment of doubt, was a part of the journey

that ultimately strengthened us. Throughout it all, I've always prioritized Elias's well-being, ensuring he felt loved and supported. The road hasn't been easy, and there were many times when I questioned whether I was doing the right thing. But in the end, the bond we share has proven strong enough to withstand the trials we've faced, demonstrating the strength we developed along the way.

One such trial occurred on Elias's 29th birthday when an unsettling incident shook both of us. His biological father, with whom he had almost no relationship, unexpectedly showed up at Elias's house early in the morning, around 6 or 7 a.m. This man had been largely absent from Elias's life—he never truly co-parented with me, never involved himself in Elias's upbringing, and only met Elias briefly without ever establishing regular visitation.

The situation was unnerving; someone who had no place in his life suddenly appeared at his home without warning, especially at such an early hour; it was not just inappropriate—it was downright alarming.

Elias immediately called me, furious and deeply unsettled by the encounter. I could hear the anger in his voice as he expressed his disbelief at his father's audacity to show up like that. Being in a different state then, I couldn't be there in person to support him, so I did my best to calm him down over the phone. He was livid, and rightfully so. The intrusion was not just a physical one but an emotional one as well, stirring up old wounds that Elias had long since tried to heal from.

Elias clarified that his father was fortunate things didn't escalate further. The tension of the moment, combined with the fact that Elias was legally armed, could have led to a much more dangerous outcome. The whole situation felt like a typical move from someone trying to exert control in a passive-aggressive way—a characteristic trait of narcissistic behavior.

This incident clearly highlights why Elias has kept his distance from his father all these years. It wasn't just about the lack of a relationship; it was about protecting himself from someone who had never truly been a part of his life yet tried to manipulate situations for his gain. Elias had long recognized that his father's sporadic attempts at involvement were less about genuine interest and more about maintaining control. The inconsistency and emotional turmoil his father brought into his life only reinforced Elias's decision to keep him at arm's length, prioritizing his well-being over a toxic connection.

Chapter 7: The Familiar Trap- Falling for Another Narcissist

"People often pretend to be someone they aren't to get what they want"

-Nicholas Sparks.

The first time I met my husband, Dan, was in a strictly professional context. I had just taken a job working under his supervision, and he naturally presented himself in a business-like, formal manner. At that time, we were both married to other people, which kept our interactions strictly professional. There was no immediate spark of romance, lingering glances, or butterflies—more like a box of office supplies than a box of chocolates. However, looking back, I realize that even in that initial meeting, there were subtle signs of what was to come. Narcissists are known for carefully selecting their victims, often choosing those who appear young, naive, or vulnerable.

Reflecting on our first interaction, it seems there must have been something about me—perhaps my inexperience or demeanor—that marked me as a suitable target for his narcissistic tendencies. The interview itself was not typical; he barely glanced at my resume and didn't ask any questions about my background or qualifications. Instead, he quickly shifted to discuss my salary expectations and start date. Having been through a few interviews before, I found it odd that he didn't inquire about my accounting skills or experience. This lack of genuine engagement left me with a sense that something was off, even if I couldn't pinpoint what it was at the time.

I still remember the interview clearly; it was a straightforward encounter, lacking the usual probing questions or attempts to establish a personal connection. I didn't think, "Oh, he's attractive," or felt drawn to his looks or charm. It was another day at the office, interacting with someone in a position of authority who was there to evaluate my professional skills.

There may have been something beneath the surface that initially drew me to him, but it wasn't the usual factors like physical appearance or charisma. My first impression of him was relatively neutral. I recall a close friend who often pointed out that I seem drawn to men in positions of power. Her observations made me reflect on my past relationships and the types of men I found myself attracted to. Over time, I noticed that I tended to be more attracted to men who held authoritative positions. These men reminded me of a father figure, offering a sense of security and control that I subconsciously sought.

This realization wasn't something I consciously recognized at the time. It took years of reflecting on my past to see the recurring pattern. My father, who started his own business when I was young, was someone I admired deeply for his drive and ambition. The men I later found myself drawn to often shared these qualities—older, more established, and possessing some level of authority. In this way, my husband fits the description almost perfectly, being 18 years older than me and in an authoritative role at the company where we worked together. His presence seemed to mirror the qualities I had grown up admiring, making him a natural figure of attraction.

As we continued to work closely together, I began to develop what I believed to be a genuine friendship with him. It felt natural and even comforting to have someone in the workplace who showed an interest in my well-being and professional growth. His attention and apparent concern for me created a sense of ease and trust I didn't question at the time. I saw our interactions as the beginning of a real connection, mistaking the comfort I felt for actual safety. Little did I know, this comfort was a sign of a deeper, more complicated dynamic developing beneath the surface.

It wasn't until years later, after reading *"The Body Keeps the Score"* by Bessel van der Kolk, that I began to understand the subconscious patterns influencing my choices. The book explains how our bodies hold on to memories of trauma and how we are often unconsciously drawn to situations and people that echo our early experiences, even if those experiences were unhealthy. This insight struck a deep chord with me. The initial excitement I felt around him, which I had interpreted as attraction, was more likely my body's way of signaling familiarity, even if that familiarity was rooted in unhealthy dynamics. This recognition was both enlightening and unsettling, challenging my previous perceptions.

The butterflies I experienced around him were not indicators of love or affection but were warnings. This was a powerful revelation because society often promotes the idea that butterflies are a positive sign indicating love or excitement. In reality, these feelings can be signals that something is amiss. Recognizing this allowed me to reframe my understanding of those initial feelings and question their true nature.

Women are often said to possess strong intuition, but we are not always encouraged to listen to it. Instead, we are taught to doubt our feelings and instincts and rely on logic and reason over our bodies' subtle signals. This societal conditioning can lead us to ignore warnings that are meant to protect us. If I had been more in tune with my intuition, I might have recognized the red flags earlier. Perhaps I would have questioned the unease I sometimes felt and taken a more cautious approach, evaluating the situation more critically before becoming emotionally involved.

Reflecting on my past relationships, this lack of listening to my intuition became even more evident. The differences between Elias's biological father, Fern, and my second husband, Dan, couldn't have been starker. Elias's father didn't work or provide for us, leaving me to carry the entire burden alone. Meeting Dan was a vivid contrast because he was a businessman who supported his family. His neat, clean, and organized nature made him seem dependable. This appealed to me, as it mirrored the stability I craved after the chaos of my first marriage. Dan's characteristics brought a sense of familiarity and comfort, reminding me of the well-ordered environment I had grown up with, which made him appealing.

Growing up, my mother was obsessive about appearances. Our house was always immaculate, with everything in its place, reflecting her almost excessive attention to cleanliness. Her standards extended to how we presented ourselves, ensuring we always dressed neatly and looked put together. It wasn't about comfort but projecting a certain image to the outside world. This upbringing shaped my understanding of a well-ordered life. It also influenced my attraction to Dan, whose similar obsession with order and presentation made me feel like I was in a familiar environment.

Dan mirrored these behaviors in his daily life. Even on weekends, when most people would take the opportunity to relax and unwind, he maintained a meticulously polished appearance. He would get up, get dressed, wet his hair, and make sure he looked presentable, regardless of having no plans to leave the house. In contrast, I preferred lounging in my pajamas, letting my hair be, and taking it easy on those days. I couldn't understand why he felt the need to dress up on a Saturday. At the time, I brushed it off as one of his quirky habits.

Now, looking back, I see it was more about maintaining an image than finding comfort or relaxation. Dan's need to appear put-together at all times went beyond personal preference; it was about projecting a certain image to the outside world, even if there was no one to see it. His behavior reminded me of the proverb, *"All that glitters is not gold."* On the surface, his meticulousness appeared admirable, but it masked deeper issues. This compulsion to uphold appearances was an indication of his need for control and perfection. I didn't see it then, but this behavior was a red flag, hinting at his underlying issues with narcissism and his constant concern with how others perceived him. His outward perfection was just a facade, like a shiny coat of paint hiding the rust underneath, concealing the complexities and darker aspects of his true personality.

There were other signs that I failed to recognize as red flags at the time. A clear hint was how Dan handled his marriage. As we became closer, I was upfront with my husband, telling him I wanted a divorce because I wasn't interested in cheating; I wanted a clean break. Dan, on the other hand, told me he was getting a divorce, claiming that his wife had been unfaithful. He painted a picture of a failing marriage to justify our involvement. However, his words didn't match his actions. It became clear later that his marriage wasn't as troubled as he had led me to believe, showing his willingness to manipulate the truth to serve his needs.

At one point, Dan said he wanted to try to make things work with his wife. I was firm in my response, telling him that if he wanted to go back to his wife, then we were done. I refused to be the other woman, the secret affair on the side. I told him to give his marriage the effort it deserved but that I wouldn't be a part of it. This didn't sit well with him.

Narcissists don't like to lose control or be told no. He kept trying to come into my office, closing the door behind him, pushing boundaries. I would make him open the door, standing my ground, telling him that if he was going to stay with his wife, then he needed to leave me alone.

Things escalated when Dan, possibly at his wife's insistence or perhaps his own, wanted me to leave the company. He called me into the office on a Saturday to tell me that I could no longer work there. My anger flared. I was a single mother, and I depended on my job. I told him bluntly that he couldn't fire me just because our relationship was ending. I made it clear that trying to terminate my employment under these circumstances was sexual harassment. I told him I could work there and not interact with him if necessary, but I wasn't going to lose my job over this. My child's needs came first, and I wasn't going to compromise on that.

Dan's persistence didn't end there. He continued to visit my office, telling me how much he missed me. I stood firm, repeating that unless he was divorced, there was no future for us. Eventually, he did tell his wife he wanted a divorce, and we began seeing each other more openly. By that time, I had moved out from my then-husband, Brian. Dan started staying with me sporadically. But even as our relationship progressed, I could see its unhealthy aspects. Dan's need for control and manipulation, his obsession with appearances, and the lies he had told all pointed to deeper issues.

Pondering those times, I realized I was just 25 and trying to find my way through complicated emotions and situations. I was still learning about myself and what I truly wanted. The environment I had grown up in had conditioned me to see certain behaviors as normal, even desirable. It took time and experience to understand that what I was attracted to wasn't always what was best for me. My attraction to Dan stemmed from a desire for stability and order, qualities he seemed to offer. But beneath those qualities was a need to control and manipulate, traits I didn't fully understand until much later.

When we were together, Dan had a habit of picking at things, deliberately saying or doing things that he knew would upset me. I remember asking him directly, "Why do you keep doing this? I've told you these things upset me, and yet you keep pushing my buttons." His behavior was deliberate, calculated even to provoke a reaction. Looking back, it's like pieces of a puzzle falling into place—realizing I didn't understand what was happening at the time. My son and I have a saying: "You don't know what you don't know." It vibrates with the confusion I felt in those moments, highlighting how unaware I was of his manipulative tendencies.

I had a sense that something was off, but I couldn't identify why these behaviors were happening. It was only later, through reflection and more understanding, that I began to see the patterns. I recognized similar traits in another man I dated, and it became clear that my husband was a covert narcissist. In fact, he was probably high on the spectrum, bordering on psychopathy. He was skilled at manipulation, turning it into an art form, knowing exactly how to twist situations. His ability to manipulate was both impressive and frightening, making it clear why covert narcissists are often considered some of the most dangerous individuals to be involved with.

Dan would often pick fights seemingly out of nowhere. I sometimes wondered if he wanted to push me to my breaking point, perhaps even to get rid of me or find a reason to fire me. There were instances at work where, during a disagreement, he would call the police, claiming I was causing a disturbance. The officers would arrive, and I'd find myself in disbelief, asking, "Am I really causing a disturbance?" It felt like a crazy game where the rules kept changing. Dan's behavior was baffling, and it left me questioning my own sanity at times, making me doubt my perception of reality.

My past experiences with my mother and my son's father undoubtedly shaped how I perceived this relationship. My mother's reaction when she saw the bruises on my arms— asking what I had done to deserve them—echoed the blame-shifting I experienced with Dan. The abuse was somehow turned around to make me seem like the problem. My mother's inability to support me reinforced the idea that I was to blame, an idea that Dan skillfully manipulated. In retrospect, it wasn't just physical abuse; it was a psychological game of control, one that I had been unknowingly trained to play from childhood, feeling like I was always in the wrong.

One of Dan's favorite tactics was love bombing. In the beginning, he showered me with attention, taking me out to dinner and making sex a major focus of our relationship. Narcissists often use sex as a tool for control, and Dan was no different. His sexual appetite was insatiable, making it seem like constant physical intimacy was a sign of love. As someone with an anxious attachment style, I misinterpreted this as affection, believing that this was how love was shown. It made me feel wanted and valued, like a person starving for water in a desert. This intensity made it easy to overlook his manipulative tendencies, as I was caught up in the whirlwind of emotions.

My past with Elias's father, who had been abusive and forced himself on me, probably made me more susceptible to Dan's manipulations. Dan didn't force me, but his schemes were more subtle, using passive aggression to achieve his goals. If he wanted to be with other women and avoid intimacy with me, he would pick fights so he had an excuse not to be close. It was a form of sexual weaponization, playing mind games that left me questioning my worth and value. If he wanted sex and I wasn't in the mood, his response was passive-aggressive, reminding me of the constant threat of infidelity and keeping me in a state of insecurity. The underlying fear that he might look elsewhere if I didn't comply made me feel like I was constantly walking on eggshells. This created a power dynamic where my choices were overshadowed by his desires, making it clear that my needs were secondary to maintaining his satisfaction and control over the relationship.

He would often say, "If a man isn't getting it at home, he'll get it somewhere else." This became a mantra, a continuous reminder that my compliance was necessary to keep him faithful. The underlying message was clear: if I didn't meet his needs, he would seek satisfaction elsewhere. It was another layer of manipulation, using fear of abandonment to control my actions. This form of mind control was effective, convincing me that my worth was tied to how well I could meet his needs. It played on my insecurities and reinforced the belief that I had to earn love by constantly pleasing him, creating an unhealthy cycle.

In the beginning, Dan was the perfect partner, taking me out to eat and showing interest in my life and my son's. He would accompany us to soccer games, becoming a part of our lives. But once we moved in together, his behavior changed drastically. He became mean to my son, showing no interest in his activities. Suddenly, he had no time for soccer games, dismissing them with, "I have my own kids." The transformation was shocking like Dr. Jekyll turning into Mr. Hyde. His love and attention were conditional, based on what he could gain from the relationship, revealing his true nature when his needs were no longer met.

Our dinners out, once enjoyable, became transactional. If we went out, I was expected to pay or at least contribute. The love bombing had ended, replaced by a cold, calculating approach to everything. It was a complete turnaround from how things had started. The gifts and compliments disappeared, and I was left wondering where the man I had fallen for had gone. It should have been a clear sign to run, but I stayed, thinking things would improve. Instead of leaving, I spent 24 years trying to make a dysfunctional relationship work, losing myself in the process, hoping against hope for a change that never came.

My upbringing, with its focus on appearances and blame-shifting, conditioned me to accept behavior that should have been unacceptable. The lack of support from my mother, combined with the abuse from Elias's father, made me vulnerable to Dan's manipulations. His covert narcissism and manipulative tactics were familiar, echoing the dysfunction I had grown up with. It wasn't just about love or affection; it was about control, power, and maintaining a facade that hid the reality of who he was. My understanding of love had been warped by my past experiences.

These experiences have taught me valuable lessons about recognizing red flags and understanding the dynamics of unhealthy relationships. I've learned that it's essential to look beyond surface-level traits and question the motivations behind them. As Maya Angelou famously said, *"When someone shows you who they are, believe them the first time."* Not everything that appears good is truly good for you. It's often the things we overlook, the behaviors we dismiss as quirks, that hold the most significance. By learning to trust my instincts and see beyond the surface, I have gained the strength to set healthier boundaries. These lessons have been hard-earned, but they are the foundation upon which I am rebuilding a life of authenticity and self-respect.

Chapter 8: Living on Eggshells-The Reality of a Narcissistic Marriage

In my marriage, daily life was a mix of responsibilities and underlying tension that often left me feeling anxious and on edge. My second husband, Dan, worked long hours, so my day typically began early, making him breakfast before he left for work. Afterward, I would take my son to school, care for our dogs, and manage the household. This included overseeing the care of his son from a previous marriage, Dan Junior, who lived with us after suffering a traumatic brain injury from a car accident years before I met Dan. Managing Dan Junior's care was demanding, involving hiring aides and coordinating with roommates. It was all on my shoulders since Dan was rarely involved in these matters. He expected me to handle everything, leaving me to juggle my job and household responsibilities without his support.

The emotional toll of these expectations was overwhelming. I felt like a tightrope walker, constantly balancing on a thin line stretched between responsibility and exhaustion, with no safety net to catch me if I fell. Each day felt like an impossible balancing act, where one misstep could send everything crashing down. "Does he not see everything I do for this family?" I would ask myself in moments of frustration.

Everyday routines like preparing dinner highlighted the expectations Dan had for me. He expected a meal on the table each evening, not necessarily at a fixed time, but my cooking was still an unspoken requirement. When he came home from work, I constantly needed to ensure the house was in perfect order. He would never outright criticize if something was amiss like laundry being left out or dishes not being done. Instead, he used passive-aggressive comments that made me feel inadequate. He might say, "Were you too busy on the computer or chatting with friends to put the laundry away?" Such remarks, though seemingly casual, made me feel like I wasn't doing enough, no matter how hard I worked.

A particularly stressful aspect of our marriage was the challenge of spending quality time together. I often suggested we take a vacation, or at least spend a day together, away from the daily grind. Dan would agree, but only after my repeated requests. When the day arrived, he would suddenly find an excuse to go to work, claiming he needed to handle a few urgent tasks. This behavior, often referred to as "future faking," was a repeated theme in our relationship. Future faking is a manipulative tactic where someone makes promises about the future without the intention of following through, giving the other person false hope and a sense of security. Dan used this tactic effectively, making me believe our time together mattered to him.

By promising these plans, he kept me holding on, thinking things would get better and he genuinely wanted to spend time with me. The reality, however, was that his promises were empty, designed to keep me from expressing my dissatisfaction or pushing for change. When the time came to fulfill those promises, he would always find a way to back out, leaving me feeling deceived and let down. His consistent failure to follow through not only eroded my trust but also made me question my worth in his eyes. Each broken promise deepened my feelings of isolation and disappointment. I would get upset, naturally hurt by his lack of commitment to our relationship, and Dan would then use my emotional reaction as an excuse to blame me, saying my upset ruined the day, and he'd return to work.

This manipulative cycle became all too familiar, with him offering hope and then snatching it away, making me feel as if my desire for connection and togetherness was unreasonable. Over time, I learned that his promises were not sincere attempts to bond or show affection but tools to keep me quiet and compliant. It was his way of avoiding conflict, making it appear like he was a caring partner while ensuring that his priorities, primarily work and control, always came first.

My anxiety and hyper-vigilance were continuous companions, especially when Dan was due to return home from work to our patio home, the first place we lived together before Danny, my stepson, got sick and eventually had to be placed in a nursing home. I would go through the house, ensuring everything was spotless and nothing was out of place. I wanted to avoid any passive-aggressive comments that would hint at my perceived failures. I felt like I was always waiting for the next comment or criticism, always preparing for his dissatisfaction. His behavior left me perpetually tense, uncertain of when the next critical or dismissive comment would emerge. The smallest things could set off a chain reaction of stress, as I worried about how he would perceive my efforts. 'Is this what marriage is supposed to feel like?' I would ask myself. 'Is it normal to feel so alone when you're not actually alone?' Considering these feelings, I recall the words of Anais Nin, *'We don't see things as they are, we see them as we are,'* which reminded me that the continuous tension and fear of criticism clouded my perception of our marriage.

There was a pervasive sense of being taken for granted. Dan's work always took priority over our relationship. He had no problem staying late at the office or bringing work home, but any suggestion of spending time together was considered a nuisance or inconvenience. This attitude made me feel like an afterthought in my marriage, a feeling that was deeply hurtful. I craved genuine connection and companionship, but those needs were consistently overshadowed by his dedication to work and disinterest in nurturing our relationship.

In retrospect, I see how my constant state of anxiety was not just a reaction to Dan's behavior but a symptom of the power dynamics in our relationship. I was responsible for maintaining the household, caring for his son, and managing my professional life while trying to keep the peace with Dan. He maintained control by keeping me off-balance, using his passive-aggressive remarks and unfulfilled promises to keep me uncertain. This manipulation made me question my worth and abilities, creating a cycle of stress and self-doubt.

The anxiety I felt was compounded by Dan's use of gaslighting and emotional manipulation, which were common tools of control in our relationship. He would often twist the truth or deny things that had happened, leaving me confused and questioning my reality. A harrowing memory is of an argument that escalated quickly. Dan, in a fit of anger, first threw water at me and then hurled a hard plastic cup, hitting me on the head. The impact of the cup left me stunned and crying, my mind racing with disbelief and hurt. But when I confronted him, asking why he would throw something at me, he denied it, saying he didn't know what I was talking about. His flat-out denial wasn't just about the act of throwing the cup; it was an intentional move to make me doubt my perception and reality, a classic gaslighting tactic that left me questioning my sanity.

This form of denial was habitual, not exceptional. Dan would typically deny any accusations of physical aggression, such as hitting, pushing, or slapping, even during reconciliatory conversations. His typical responses, "I never hit you," or "I just stopped you from pushing me," were efforts to rewrite reality, confusing and isolating me further. These persistent denials eroded my confidence in my memories, ensuring I remained unsure and dependent. This tactic effectively kept me in a state of continual uncertainty about both my experiences and my responses to them, profoundly affecting my ability to trust myself and my interpretations of our interactions.

Dan's manipulation also manifested in how he administered physical abuse, cleverly calculated to minimize visible evidence. He would often employ force in a way that avoided leaving marks, like dragging me off the bed or downstairs, causing pain without visible injury. On one occasion, he pulled me down the stairs by my foot, causing severe back injuries. When we visited the doctor, Dan preempted my explanation by fabricating a story about me slipping and falling, which he presented as an unfortunate accident he couldn't prevent. This not only concealed the abuse but also publicly repositioned him as a helper rather than a perpetrator.

Throughout our 25 years together, the stress from these abusive dynamics took a toll on my physical health, causing my weight to fluctuate drastically. When stress levels were at their highest, I would lose my appetite entirely and become frighteningly thin. In contrast, when the stress wasn't as intense but still ever-present, I would gain weight despite not eating well. I suspect this was due to high levels of cortisol, a stress hormone known to cause various issues with metabolism. These changes in my weight were not just physical symptoms; they were clear signs of the emotional turmoil I was going through.

After a year of living together, I couldn't handle how he treated my son, so I moved out and bought my own house. This step should have ended our relationship, as it clearly showed his unacceptable behavior. However, I returned to him a decision I still can't fully understand. Returning to him didn't ease the stress; it made things worse. It was like I was drawn back into the same toxic environment that had caused me so much pain before.

The years that followed were filled with ever-increasing anxiety. We had a long break where we lived apart, but the same old patterns emerged when we reunited and moved back together. He would often brush off my feelings, suggesting that my anxiety was just a mental health issue that needed medication. I have always been someone who prefers holistic approaches and avoids pharmaceuticals whenever possible. Despite this, his constant pressure and the overwhelming nature of my anxiety led me to start taking anti-anxiety medication. This decision was not what I wanted and went against my beliefs. His insistence on medication highlighted a bigger problem in our relationship: his lack of respect for my personal beliefs and boundaries.

Starting the medication was a turning point. I had hoped it would help reduce some of the mental strain, but it did the opposite, making my anxiety even worse. Then, I read a revealing article in Forbes magazine that criticized these medications, saying they often don't work unless the anxiety is due to specific chemical imbalances. The article described how these medications sometimes act more like placebos, offering minimal real benefit. This information was eye-opening and confirmed what I had begun to suspect: that the medication wasn't truly helping me.

The process of coming off the medication was incredibly tough. I experienced severe vertigo, nausea, and other withdrawal symptoms that left me debilitated for days. My husband's reaction during this time was anything but supportive. He accused me of being lazy and pretending to be sick, showing a complete lack of empathy. His reaction during my withdrawal period highlighted the toxic nature of our relationship. His absence of support during my most challenging moments reinforced the emotional cruelty that had been present throughout much of our marriage. This difficult period not only tested my physical and emotional strength but also made it clear how little compassion existed in our relationship.

Despite these hardships, stopping the medication was a vital step toward reclaiming my health and autonomy. Although I still experienced anxiety, it wasn't made worse by medication side effects or by feeling like I had betrayed my own beliefs about treatment. This experience taught me to trust my instincts about my health and to rely on holistic approaches that align with my values. I realized I needed to take charge of my well-being and not let my partner undermine my perceptions or choices. Coming through this challenging time, I felt more empowered and committed to my health than ever before, ready to prioritize my needs and well-being.

My husband's jealousy and passive-aggressive behavior played a significant role in cutting me off from my friends and family. He didn't forbid me from seeing them directly, but he clarified that he wasn't interested in being part of my family life. For example, he rarely joined me when I visited my parents, except on major holidays. It was normal for couples to visit together in my family, but Dan always had an excuse. He would say he needed to work, stay home, or have other things to do. This made me uncomfortable and created tension. I often wondered if he was trying to discourage me from seeing my parents, but I kept visiting them anyway. However, his absence during family events led to questions from my family, adding to the strain.

When Dan did come to family gatherings, his behavior was far from supportive. After spending time with my brothers and sisters, he would criticize them and find fault with everything they did. He would complain for weeks afterward, much like my mother used to do, picking apart each of my family members. I would think to myself, "These are people I love. How can he judge them so harshly after only spending a few hours with them?" His comments created a divide, making me feel like I had to choose between my family and keeping peace at home. This was his way of isolating me, turning my support system into a source of conflict.

Dan's controlling nature also affected my friendships. He knew that I valued my friends and enjoyed spending time with them. However, he would often interfere with my plans. If I made plans to go out with friends, he would suddenly say he was free that night and wanted to spend time with me. Sometimes, this led to us spending time together, but more often, it was just a way to make me cancel my plans. Over time, I found myself seeing my friends less and less. He never told me directly not to see them, but his actions slowly led to my friendships fading. By the time our marriage was fully established, I had lost touch with almost all my friends.

This isolation became even more pronounced when his health declined, and his behavior took a turn for the worse. His passive-aggressive tactics turned into open hostility. His jealousy became more apparent, and he started acting out more aggressively. When we moved to South Dakota, being physically distant from my friends and family made me feel even more isolated. I lived on 13 acres with him, and all the tasks of maintaining the property fell on me. I remember spending hours mowing the lawn, only to come inside and face his anger. He would yell at me, demanding when dinner would be ready and criticizing my efforts. "Why are you wasting time mowing the lawn?" he would shout. "This place is a mess anyway."

Dan's behavior worsened notably after he developed dementia. His already tricky behavior turned into outright cruelty. What had been passive aggression became direct verbal and physical abuse. One time, he punched me in the lip, causing it to bleed. I was in shock and ended up calling my son, who then called the police. It was a chaotic scene, and looking back, it's surprising he didn't end up in jail that night. The police saw his mental state and chose not to arrest him, understanding he was not fully aware of his actions. Despite everything, I stood up for him, knowing he had dementia yet feeling conflicted about whether he deserved the consequences.

As his dementia progressed, it became more apparent that his cruel behavior wasn't just because of the disease; it had always been part of who he was. I thought back to my mother, who also had dementia. When I visited her, she was always happy to see me, full of love and joy, even if she thought it had been years since our last visit. In contrast, Dan's dementia seemed to bring out more anger and hostility, reinforcing the realization that he had never truly cared for me. His illness stripped away any pretense, revealing the true nature of his behavior.

As Dan's mental state worsened, I began discovering things about our life together that shocked me. I learned he had been unfaithful for years, probably throughout our entire marriage. This betrayal was devastating. I also discovered he had bought properties without my knowledge, making major financial decisions behind me. These discoveries shattered any remaining illusions I had about our relationship. I began to see our life together as a series of lies and control tactics. Realizing that he had been deceitful for so long left me questioning everything about our marriage. I couldn't help but feel foolish for not seeing it sooner, yet I also understood how skilled he had been at hiding his true self.

These discoveries pushed me to seek out support and understanding. I started talking to a spiritual mentor, trying to make sense of my experiences and come to terms with what I had been through. The more I spoke, the clearer it became that my marriage had been filled with manipulation and control. I began to understand the nature of emotional abuse, realizing that I had been enduring it for years. Opening up about my experiences was like lifting a weight off my shoulders. Once I acknowledged the truth, I couldn't ignore it anymore. I felt anger, sadness, relief, and a sense of betrayal. Most importantly, I felt a growing strength and determination to move forward and reclaim my life.

Coming to terms with the reality of my marriage was a difficult but necessary step. It allowed me to start rebuilding my life on my terms. I realized that the isolation I had felt was not my doing but a result of deliberate actions taken to keep me under control. As I reflected on my situation, the words of Eleanor Roosevelt came to mind: *"No one can make you feel inferior without your consent."* Understanding this truth was empowering. It reminded me that while I couldn't change the past, I could reclaim my power and refuse to let Dan's manipulation define my future.

Chapter 9: The Awakening- Recognizing Narcissistic Abuse

I had always known something was off, a missing piece in the emotional puzzle that was my marriage, but it took a chakra class to bring everything into focus. When the instructor mentioned that people with narcissistic personality disorder often have a closed heart chakra, it felt like a jolt of electricity ran through me. It was as if she had handed me the key to understanding years of confusion and hurt. My husband's emotional distance, his lack of affection, suddenly clicked into place. The idea that he was unable to genuinely love because his heart was, in a sense, closed off explained so much. In that instant, I realized his emotional void wasn't just a minor quirk or a result of his upbringing; it was a fundamental part of who he was, shaping every aspect of our relationship.

For years, I had tried to rationalize my husband's emotional detachment by suspecting he might have Asperger's due to his lack of emotional expression. He was always so distant, never showing excitement, joy, or sadness. I often wondered if I was at fault or if I was overreacting to the situation. The explanation of a closed heart chakra deeply affected me, providing much-needed clarity and validating my feelings. This understanding was both painful and freeing, allowing me to finally see the situation for what it truly was.

The chakra class inspired me to start researching narcissistic abuse. I felt compelled to understand more about what I was experiencing. My initial search was broad, starting with social media, where I found posts from others sharing similar experiences. It was comforting to know that I wasn't alone and that others had felt the same emotional void in their relationships. This realization pushed me to look for more substantial resources, leading me to experts who specialized in narcissistic abuse. I needed to dig deeper to understand why I felt the way I did and to begin making sense of my emotions and experiences.

As I searched for answers, I came across the work of Sam Vaknin, which changed how I understood my marriage. Vaknin's insights into narcissistic personality disorder shed light on the behaviors I had observed but struggled to explain. His discussions about the absence of empathy and the ways narcissists manipulate others struck a chord with my own experiences. It was as if he was describing my husband directly, putting into words the painful reality I had been living. Vaknin's content helped me see the truth of my relationship, making it impossible to continue denying the nature of my husband's behavior. I realized my husband's actions were not just signs of emotional detachment or a reserved personality. Instead, they were indicative of a deeper issue related to narcissism. This understanding provided much-needed clarity, allowing me to see the emotional distance and lack of genuine connection for what they truly were.

Alongside Vaknin, I found the work of Dr. Ramani Durvasula, whose insights into narcissistic abuse were equally impactful. Her book, *"It's Not You,"* provided a thorough explanation of narcissistic behavior and its effects on those who endure it. As I read her descriptions, I felt an intense sense of recognition. The emotional disconnection, the subtle manipulations, and the constant feeling of being gaslighted were all too familiar. It made me realize that the problem was not with me but with the abusive nature of narcissism. This awareness was vital in my healing process, allowing me to see my experiences more clearly and begin to recover.

As I probed deeper into these expert perspectives, I realized that social media had played a crucial role in my early understanding of narcissistic abuse. It was through these platforms that I found a sense of community and validation, reading stories from others who had experienced similar emotional voids. The online content acted as a stepping stone, guiding me toward more credible sources like Sam Vaknin and Dr. Ramani Durvasula. While social media provided a feeling of solidarity, it was the expert insights that offered the real depth of understanding I needed. These resources helped me start piecing together the reality of my situation and recognize the true nature of the emotional abuse I had endured.

I continued to learn more about narcissism and reflect on my marriage; I was not prepared for the next revelation that would come to light. The discovery that my husband, Dan, had been unfaithful hit me hard, and it came at a time when he was already struggling with dementia. It all started when I decided to take his phone away. He had his phone with him in memory care for quite a while, but it had become a source of frustration for him. He was constantly losing it, forgetting where he had placed it, and then getting upset about it. One day, I decided to take the phone away for good, thinking he wouldn't even notice its absence. While going through the process of backing up his phone, I stumbled upon old text messages that left me shaken. The texts were to and from various people whose names I didn't recognize, and the content hinted at affairs. It was at that moment I felt like my entire world had collapsed. I realized that the man I had loved and the life we had built together might have all been based on lies and deception.

As I read through more of those messages, a mix of emotions began to wash over me—anger, betrayal, confusion, and immense grief. I felt like I had been living a lie for years, investing my love and energy into a relationship that was never what I believed it to be. The awareness that Dan had been deceiving me was mind-blowing. It felt like a punch to the gut, making me question everything I had believed about our marriage. How could I not have seen this? How could I have been so blind to the reality of what was happening right in front of me? The shock of it all was overwhelming, and I found myself grappling with so many questions. But Dan's dementia meant there were no answers. Even if I confronted him, he wouldn't have the clarity or the memory to explain.

The lack of answers made it difficult to process my emotions. I couldn't confront Dan, couldn't ask him why he did what he did, or even get any acknowledgment of his actions. There was a part of me that felt it might have been easier if he had been able to explain, to provide some reasoning, even if it was just a denial. At least then, I would have had something to work with, some way to make sense of everything. The silence, the inability to confront him, left me feeling stuck in my grief and anger, unable to move forward. I found myself alternating between deep sadness and intense anger, mourning the years of my life that felt wasted on someone who didn't truly care about me.

To cope with the overwhelming emotions, I turned to my spiritual mentor and an energy worker. They became a lifeline, helping me address the sea of pain and confusion I was drowning in. Through various therapies and healing sessions, I began to peel back the layers of trauma that had built up over the years. It was a long and difficult process, filled with moments of doubt and despair. Some days, the pain felt unbearable, and the betrayal was too deep to overcome. But little by little, I started to find ways to accept what had happened. I learned to show compassion to myself, to my past self, who had loved Dan and believed in him. I realized that I couldn't blame myself for his actions. His betrayal was a reflection of him, not of me or my worth.

The journey of healing was far from easy. There were days when I felt like my entire life had been in vain, years devoted to someone who could not genuinely reciprocate my affection. The sense of loss was deep—not only the loss of my husband as I had known him but also the loss of the life I thought we had built together. It felt as though I had been deprived of the chance to be with someone who truly cared for me, someone capable of returning the love I was ready to give. The regret weighed heavily on me, and the sorrow seemed without end. However, as I continued my sessions with my spiritual mentor and energy healer, I began to gradually let go of some of the pain. I learned to release the anger and bitterness in my heart. With time, this process helped me to find a sense of peace and acceptance of what had happened. I embraced the lessons learned from my experiences, which fueled my personal growth and understanding of myself and my relationships. This shift didn't happen overnight, but each step forward made me feel a bit lighter and more hopeful about the future.

In accepting what had happened, I found a sense of peace. It wasn't a quick fix, and it didn't erase the years of pain, but it allowed me to start moving forward. I focused on rebuilding my life, on finding joy in the present moment rather than dwelling on the past. I discovered that by letting go of the need for answers, I could begin to heal. I stopped seeking explanations for Dan's actions and started focusing on my own well-being. The process of healing became less about understanding why and more about learning how to live fully despite the hurt. By giving myself permission to grieve and then slowly letting go, I began to find a way to reclaim my life and my happiness.

In my marriage, the circumstances didn't involve a decision to walk away from Dan or to end our relationship, as he passed away. My son played no role in influencing a separation either. However, he has been incredibly supportive in dealing with everything that surfaced afterward. He was there for me, offering a listening ear and understanding as I processed the reality of what had happened. We used to talk a lot about past situations, trying to make sense of them. One thing my son often pointed out was my constant complaint about Dan not spending time with me. It was a recurring issue in our marriage that now, in hindsight, made perfect sense.

As my son and I reflected on the past, it became clearer why Dan had been so emotionally absent. We both recognized that Dan's behavior wasn't just aloofness but a symptom of something deeper. My son remembered questioning whether Dan even liked doing anything, or if he had any personal interests or desires. It seemed that Dan never expressed excitement or joy about any activity. The truth is that narcissists don't have a genuine sense of identity; they live through others. Dan's lack of opinions or enthusiasm was a reflection of his dependence on my reactions and emotions. If I showed excitement about something, he might mimic that enthusiasm. But if asked what he wanted to do, his typical response would always be, "Whatever you want." It wasn't about him not caring; it was about him lacking an independent sense of self.

My son and I have a close relationship, and his support has been invaluable. He's been more caring and understanding than I could have asked for, often providing comfort when I felt overwhelmed by the revelations. He's a good man, more empathetic and compassionate than Dan ever was. His support helped me see through the fog of manipulation and understand why things were the way they were. It's been a difficult journey, but having him by my side has made it more bearable.

Looking back, I can see the patterns of narcissistic behavior that were present even in my childhood. The manipulation, the subtle pressure to act a certain way, and the passive-aggressiveness were all there. It's hard to pinpoint specific incidents because they all blend into a general pattern of behavior that shaped my upbringing. The trauma bond that developed made me feel anxious when away from my mother and later from Dan. It was a cycle that repeated itself in my relationships, creating a constant need to explain myself, justify my actions, and seek approval. This need to over-explain everything started with my parents and carried through my marriage with Dan and into subsequent relationships. It's a behavior rooted in the distrust and insecurity instilled by those who manipulate and deceive.

The constant chaos of these relationships, the emotional highs and lows, the unpredictability of their moods—one minute they're happy, the next, they're irrationally angry— became a normal part of my life. It's exhausting and draining, living in a state of constant alertness, never knowing what to expect. The comprehension that these were traits of narcissistic personalities helped me understand why my relationships felt so turbulent. It wasn't about me doing something wrong; it was about the instability inherent in relationships with people who lack genuine emotional connections.

This understanding hit even harder when I was with the last guy. I began noticing behaviors and patterns that were unsettlingly familiar. The way he spoke to me, the subtle manipulations, the emotional games—it all reminded me so much of my husband, Dan. I found myself thinking, "My God, you're just like Dan." At the time, I didn't recognize these behaviors as symptoms of narcissistic personality traits. I just thought it was a strange coincidence. I wondered if it was because they were both from New York or because they were around the same age. It was mind-blowing to see so many similarities and not understand the underlying cause.

My awareness of these patterns didn't come overnight. I began my healing journey back in 2016, focusing on spiritual growth with the guidance of a mentor. At that time, my healing wasn't centered around narcissistic abuse. Instead, it revolved around dealing with my mother's dementia and my personal struggles. I was looking for peace and understanding in my life. My focus on healing took a turn in early 2022 when I switched spiritual mentors and began working with an energy healer. This new direction allowed me to start addressing deeper, older traumas, some of which dated back to my childhood.

Working with the energy healer opened up parts of my past that I had long buried or never fully understood. It was as if I was uncovering layers of my life that had been hidden under years of pain and denial. This process brought up memories and feelings that I didn't realize were affecting me. I learned about karmic patterns and began to see that many of my relationships, both in this lifetime and possibly in others, followed the same hurtful dynamics. These insights were eye-opening and helped me understand why I kept attracting similar people into my life.

I engaged in various healing practices, including what some refer to as "journeys," where I used drumming and meditation to explore past lives and the current life I was living. I had vivid experiences that showed me past interactions with my mother, the man I had recently been involved with, my oldest brother, and Dan. These experiences revealed repeated patterns of trauma and conflict that spanned lifetimes. According to my energy healer, the recent relationship was a continuation of many past lifetimes where we had been locked in cycles of pain— sometimes, I was the one hurting him, and other times, he was hurting me.

It's easy to say, "It's all their fault," but part of my healing was about recognizing my behavior and choices. I needed to understand why I was drawn to people who treated me this way and why I accepted it. The saying "It takes two to tango" doesn't excuse abusive behavior, but it highlights the need for self-reflection. I had to take accountability for my part in these relationships, not in a way that blamed me for the abuse, but in a way that helped me learn and grow.

One of my challenges has been my tendency to overtake accountability. I've often found myself assuming responsibility not only for my actions but also for the actions of others. This tendency led me to blame myself for things that were beyond my control, including the abusive behaviors of others. Learning to set boundaries in my mind and understanding what is my responsibility and what is not has been a significant part of my healing journey. I had to learn to say, "This part is mine, but that part belongs to them." This understanding was important for my self-awareness and helped me reclaim my sense of self.

These insights have deeply influenced my relationship with my son. I've recognized the mistakes I made as a parent, even if they were unintentional. It's not about blaming myself but about acknowledging those mistakes and making amends. I've had open conversations with my son, admitting when I was wrong, and apologizing for my actions. This honesty has improved the energy between us, leading to a healthier and happier relationship. It has brought us closer together, allowing us to build a relationship based on understanding and mutual respect.

Recently, my son and I had an argument where I called him out on something he was doing. He responded by expressing how my words made him feel, bringing up feelings of frustration. I didn't respond initially because I needed time to process his feedback. Later, I apologized for not being mindful of his feelings and explained my reaction. I acknowledged his perspective and explained that my reaction was influenced by my concerns about his behavior, such as not fulfilling his work responsibilities. This dialogue was a learning experience for both of us and a testament to how far our relationship has come. It showed me that our relationship is strong enough to handle disagreements and that we can resolve conflicts through honest communication.

Reflecting on my experiences, I see why these challenging situations had to happen. They were necessary for my spiritual growth and understanding. They taught me valuable lessons about myself, my patterns, and the way I interact with others. They have helped me become more aware, more compassionate, and more in tune with my needs and boundaries. I've learned that healing is not about blaming others or oneself but about understanding, accepting, and growing. It's about breaking cycles and creating healthier, more fulfilling relationships.

Chapter 10: The Relapse: Falling Back into Old Patterns

In November 2022, I met Andrew, who would eventually become an important yet brief chapter in my life. He worked for the company responsible for maintenance in the community where I owned a home in Florida. I used to frequent a tiki bar near my home, where I often talked to the bartender, where I first encountered Andrew. At the time, my husband, Dan, had been placed in a memory care facility a few months earlier in August, and I was still processing the emotional weight of that decision. Although I had been aware that Dan was a narcissist, I didn't yet understand the full extent of his behavior. I was lonely, vulnerable, and still coming to terms with my reality.

The initial attraction was physical when I first saw Andrew at the tiki bar. He was standing there, talking about something I barely paid attention to, as I wasn't overly interested in what he said. I responded sarcastically, joking that he should remove his shirt because that's how I hire people. He did, and I realized I was drawn to his appearance. He was older, which I had always preferred, and had tattoos, which added to the attraction.

At that point, I wasn't looking for anything serious, just someone to have fun with and distract me from my situation. I invited Andrew to meet me again the next day, even though I didn't know his exact schedule because he worked irregular hours. The next day, I returned to the tiki bar, had lunch, and waited for him to show up. When he arrived, his behavior was crass and lacking any sense of refinement. He made inappropriate and offhanded comments, but I chose to overlook them. My focus was entirely on escaping my loneliness, and I didn't care much about his character. In that moment, companionship, however shallow, seemed more important than confronting the red flags in his behavior.

One thing that initially set Andrew apart from other people I had been involved with, especially my late husband, was his effort to appear polished. On our first night out, he arrived at my house with flowers and a bottle of wine, dressed up like he was trying to impress me. This clearly contrasts Dan, who would never have done something like that. In fact, one early incident with Dan still stands out in my memory and was a clear sign of the unhealthy dynamics in our relationship.

When Dan and I had been seeing each other for only a few months, an argument escalated quickly. It took place in my apartment, upstairs in my bedroom. I can't recall exactly what we were arguing about, but I remember vividly how he reacted. As a bit of background, my first husband and I had gone on a free cruise that my company offered, and since we were young and just starting, I had to buy fancy dresses for the evening dinners. Buying those dresses was a big deal because we didn't have much money, so I kept them in good condition, thinking I'd have them for future weddings or formal occasions.

Those dresses were hung in my closet upstairs, untouched when Dan and I argued. During that fight, Dan stormed over to my closet, grabbed all the dresses, and threw them on the floor in a rage. He yelled at me, accusing me of acting like I was someone special for owning them. He went on to say that I would never wear them, didn't deserve them, and should just throw them away. It felt like an attack on who I was and what I valued. What made it even more jarring was that I bought those dresses with my own money. At the time of the argument, Dan and I had barely been dating; this was my apartment, not his. Yet there he was, disrespectfully treating my things and belittling me for owning them.

I remember feeling a surge of anger and sadness at the same time. I yelled at him to get out of my house, tears streaming down my face. It was one of those moments where everything felt wrong. The fact that he felt entitled to treat me and my belongings like that, especially so early in the relationship, should have been a massive red flag. But at the time, I didn't recognize it for what it was—narcissistic abuse. His behavior was a way of controlling me, making me feel small and unworthy. He was trying to diminish me, to make me believe that I didn't deserve nice things, simply because he said so.

Reflecting, I now understand why I allowed this behavior to happen. Growing up in a chaotic household where arguments often escalated to things being thrown and tempers flaring, I had become desensitized to this kind of aggression. In some ways, it felt normal, even though it wasn't. My brain had come to accept this chaos as part of relationships. Additionally, with Dan being 18 years older than me, I felt an imbalance of power in our relationship. He held an authority over me that sometimes made it difficult for me to stand up for myself. I felt like I had to accept his behavior, even though it made me feel awful.

That incident with the dresses was just one example of how the dynamics in our relationship were unhealthy from the beginning. I didn't see his actions as a pattern of narcissistic abuse—behavior designed to control, belittle, and make me feel inferior. It was only later that I realized how this incident, and many others like it, were signs of a toxic relationship. Dan's actions were not just outbursts of anger; they were calculated ways to undermine my sense of self-worth.

Andrew stood out initially because he was willing to put on this facade, making it seem like he was going above and beyond, something I wasn't used to. However, it soon became clear that he couldn't maintain the polished image he had tried to present. Wanting to enjoy our evening, I picked a nice restaurant, knowing well that he couldn't afford it. I ordered food and champagne that I liked, knowing from the start that I would cover the bill. At the time, I wasn't worried about his inability to pay because I didn't see this as the beginning of a relationship. For me, this was more about enjoying a rare moment of fun—something I had been deprived of for so many years—than about evaluating him as a potential partner.

In retrospect, I realize that my longing for companionship and the excitement of being with someone who seemed so different clouded my judgment. The novelty of Andrew's rough exterior and the fact that he was giving me attention made it easy to overlook his obvious flaws, even though they were right in front of me from the start.

It's easy to see how Andrew was different from previous partners, but not in the ways that mattered. While Dan had been emotionally manipulative and narcissistic, Andrew was more transparent in his crudeness and lack of depth. He didn't try to control me like Dan—at least not in the beginning. But as time went on, I realized he did have narcissistic traits that I initially missed because of the "love bombing" phase at the start of the relationship. It had been so long since I experienced this stage that I didn't even remember it existed. The overwhelming affection and attention made it easy to overlook the subtle signs of manipulation. Andrew and I were not on the same level in many ways—socially, spiritually, or in terms of behavior— but I found myself drawn to him during a vulnerable time. I was grieving the loss of my marriage, even though Dan was still alive, and I was desperate for something, anything, that felt like a release from the loneliness I was experiencing.

The most notable difference between Andrew and other men I had been with was how quickly he moved things forward. He wasn't shy about his intentions, and there was no pretense of romance or emotional connection. Initially, it was purely physical, and I was fine with that. I wasn't looking for anything long-term or meaningful; I just wanted a distraction. But even in those early days, I sensed this wouldn't end well. As they say, "We accept the love we think we deserve," and at that time, I didn't believe I deserved more. I wanted to believe that Andrew could offer something new, something different, but in reality, he was just another version of the same type of person I had been dealing with for years. The attraction I felt was more about my need to escape my pain than Andrew himself.

The night we went out for dinner was enjoyable, but it set the stage for a toxic relationship. Toward the end of the evening, he wanted to stay the night, and I said no. Now, I understand that this likely bruised his ego, as narcissists cannot handle rejection. This was the red flag, but I didn't recognize it then. The next day, I told him I was busy, yet he showed up near my home anyway. We lived in a gated community, so he had no business being there without permission. It felt like a violation, but I dismissed the discomfort, not realizing its significance. Narcissists often test boundaries early on to see what they can get away with. He pushed those limits by showing up uninvited, and I failed to see the warning signs clearly.

As time went on, his true nature started to emerge in other, more concerning ways. One night, while in Florida, we went out with a close friend and her husband for dinner and a tribute concert. During the concert, Andrew's jealousy surfaced. My friend's husband greeted me with a hug, a simple, friendly gesture, which triggered Andrew's insecurities.

Later that night, after we returned to my house, Andrew—drunk and visibly upset—threatened to confront my friend's husband. Despite my pleading, he stormed down to their house in the middle of the night, pounding on their door and screaming at my friend's husband to 'stay away' from me. The incident embarrassed and confused me, effectively ruining my friendship. I was torn between my relationship with Andrew and the friendship I had worked hard to build. It was yet another red flag I chose to overlook at the time, too blinded by my desire for companionship.

One of the first lies he told me was about his age. I didn't realize how serious this was at the time, but it should have been another clear red flag. Narcissists often begin with small lies to test how much they can get away with. It was unsettling when I found out the truth, but I didn't understand the depth of manipulation happening. He was conditioning me to accept dishonesty, making it easier for him to lie about bigger things in the future. This was his way of gaining control over the situation.

That weekend, he told me that someone had reported him for staying at my house, claiming his truck was seen in the driveway. I wasn't sure what the rules were, but the story didn't sit right with me. Now, I see this was likely a fabricated tale to manipulate me. Narcissists often create false narratives to make their victims feel guilty or responsible for situations that aren't real. As explained in *"The Gaslight Effect"* by Dr. Robin Stern, narcissists use these tactics to distort their victims' perception of reality, making them question their judgment. He used this story to make me feel like our relationship had more consequences than it did, leaving me guilty and responsible for something that likely never happened.

I thought the solution was simple: if being with me jeopardized his job, we would stop seeing each other. But that wasn't his real goal. Andrew wasn't looking for a solution; he wanted to maintain control and keep me emotionally tied to him. Narcissists don't thrive on simple solutions—they thrive on creating chaos. By fabricating this story about his job being at risk, he wasn't seeking a way out of the problem. Instead, he was manipulating my emotions, trying to make me feel guilty and responsible for his supposed troubles. It was another tactic to keep me confused, emotionally drained, and dependent on him.

As time went on, his lies grew more elaborate. A small lie about his age quickly escalated into more complex stories. I doubted what was real and what wasn't, which is exactly what he wanted. He was testing how much I would tolerate, and I was already deep into his manipulations by the time I realized what was happening.

I later came across a class by Richard Gannon, who, although not a psychologist, has studied narcissism extensively. He explains how narcissism is like a "cult of one," where the narcissist is the leader of their mini-cult, controlling and manipulating those around them for their benefit. The class, co-hosted with Mark Vicente (known for exposing the NXIVM cult), was eye-opening. It drew connections between cult brainwashing and the behavior of narcissists. As Gannon said, *"Narcissists create their reality and expect everyone around them to live in it."*

One of the most impactful lessons I learned was the difference between gaslighting and confabulation. Gaslighting, often associated with psychopathic behavior, is when the abuser knows the truth but deliberately tries to convince you otherwise. It's a calculated form of manipulation where the abuser's goal is to make you question your reality. For example, if someone throws a cup at you and then flat-out denies it, despite both of you knowing what happened, that's gaslighting. It's a method used to distort the victim's perception of reality, leaving them feeling confused and questioning their memories. The abuser, in this case, is fully aware of the truth but intentionally alters it to undermine the victim's sense of certainty.

On the other hand, confabulation, more common with narcissists, is different in a subtle but critical way. Rather than intentionally lying, narcissist creates a false narrative in their mind to protect their fragile ego. They don't just deceive others; they deceive themselves. Narcissists genuinely believe the alternate reality they've constructed. In Andrew's case, he would rewrite events to absolve himself of any wrongdoing and place the blame on me. For instance, if something went wrong in our relationship, Andrew would convince himself that I was the problem, no matter how irrational the story became. The impact on the victim, however, is just as damaging as gaslighting, as it leaves you questioning your sanity and your role in the situation. Understanding this distinction between gaslighting and confabulation was a revelation that allowed me to better comprehend the manipulation I experienced with Andrew. It also made me reflect on my childhood, where my mother seemed to operate in a similar 'cult-like' manner, manipulating those around her to maintain control.

I did try to distance myself. When I first found out about the lie regarding his age, I ignored his messages for days, thinking that would be the end of it. But he managed to convince me that it was a harmless mistake. Like narcissists, he was an expert at making his lies seem insignificant, downplaying his actions to make me question his reactions. He knew how to push the right buttons to keep me engaged, even after I was ready to walk away.

Over time, I noticed more inconsistencies in his stories but was too caught up in the relationship to see things clearly. He made me feel guilty for questioning him, turning the tables, and making me seem unreasonable. Breaking free from him wasn't easy. I had already invested too much emotional energy when I realized what was happening. But eventually, I found the strength to walk away. Narcissists thrive on control; once you break free from that control, they lose their power. It took time and self-reflection, but I finally saw through his lies and manipulation.

Every time we went out, Andrew seemed to play a game I didn't initially recognize. Looking back, I believe he was always on the lookout for other women, constantly flirting and seeking attention from them. He smoked, and I didn't, so he would regularly step outside to have a cigarette while we were at bars or restaurants. Even though many of Florida's bars are open-air, smoking indoors is still prohibited, so he would leave me alone at the table while he went outside. During those moments, other men often approached me, sometimes sitting beside me and starting conversations. I wasn't seeking their attention, but it naturally happened, especially when Andrew wasn't around.

Initially, I couldn't understand his jealousy. If he was so concerned about other men talking to me, why was he leaving me alone in the first place? I told him that he didn't own me, and if men were interested in me, it wasn't something I had control over. His insecurity felt misplaced, but at the same time, I loved the attention I was receiving. After years of being with Dan, who rarely paid me any compliments or showed any affection, I was soaking up the attention of other men. I had been deprived of feeling desirable for so long, so being noticed was something I deeply craved.

I hadn't dressed up for years in my marriage. Even when I did put in the effort, Dan never noticed or complimented me. So, when I was out with Andrew and other men were giving me attention, it felt like validation I had long been denied. I wasn't looking to start anything with anyone else, but I enjoyed talking to these men. It gave me confidence and renewed energy I hadn't felt in decades. I didn't feel bad about it then, and even now, I don't regret enjoying that attention.

Andrew's behavior with waitresses and bartenders became increasingly noticeable. He would openly flirt with them, and it became clear that he craved attention just as much as I did. However, the key difference between us was that I was transparent about enjoying the attention I received, while Andrew's reaction was far less tolerant. Whenever someone else noticed me, he would get visibly upset, his mood shifting almost instantly. His jealousy became more intense over time, escalating from minor irritation to full-blown anger whenever I received any attention, creating an unsettling atmosphere in our relationship.

While Andrew was outside smoking one night, a man approached and sat at our table. I immediately warned him that Andrew would return soon and that he was prone to extreme jealousy, hoping the man would take the hint and leave before any issues arose. Unfortunately, the man either didn't care or didn't take my warning seriously and chose to stay. His decision to remain seated created a sense of tension I desperately wanted to avoid, knowing that Andrew would react badly to the situation upon his return.

Andrew had a habit of lurking in the background, watching me from a distance as if waiting to catch me doing something wrong. He would stand back, peeking around corners, hoping to find something to confirm his jealousy. I found this behavior both creepy and infuriating. If I was talking to someone, I wasn't hiding it. I wasn't doing anything wrong, yet his constant surveillance made me feel like I was always under a microscope. It wasn't just the jealousy that bothered me; it was how he tried to control me through this covert monitoring. I told him straight up, "Stop watching me from a distance. If you have a problem, say it to my face." His need to catch me in the act of something that wasn't happening showed just how insecure and manipulative he was.

As time went on, Andrew's jealousy became unbearable, intensifying with each outing. One night, around Christmas time, we were out at a bar, and we were drinking. I usually don't drink much, but that night felt different. I was in full party mode, celebrating the fact that the responsibilities of caregiving no longer tied me down. I felt free, almost like a kid again. Having had my son at 20, I never really got the chance to experience what people call "sowing their wild oats." There were small bursts in my life where I could let loose, but never a true stretch of freedom. This was one of those rare moments where I let my guard down and embraced the experience. I wanted to just go out, have fun, drink, dance, and enjoy the night without overthinking it. However, what started as a carefree evening quickly spiraled as Andrew's jealousy flared up again, overshadowing the fun I was trying to have.

At Whiskey Park that night, a woman kissed me at the bar, and Andrew saw it happen. His reaction was immediate and intense. He flew into a rage, not at the woman but the men around us, as if he needed someone to direct his anger toward.

He was ready to fight three random guys who had nothing to do with the situation, puffing his chest and acting aggressively. It was as if the kiss, a harmless moment, had triggered something deeper in him. I had to physically drag him out of the bar, trying to de-escalate the situation while also dealing with my disbelief at how extreme his response was. He was furious over something so trivial, something that shouldn't have mattered at all, especially since it was a woman who kissed me, not a man.

In the heat of the moment, I remember telling him sarcastically, "She actually kissed better than you." It wasn't just an offhand remark but a reflection of what I had noticed for a while. Narcissists like Andrew tend to see people as objects rather than as emotional beings. As Lundy Bancroft writes in Why Does He Do That? *"The central attitudes driving the man who chronically behaves this way are entitlement, control, and ownership."* Andrew's reaction wasn't born from genuine jealousy or concern for our relationship—it was about control. His rage felt more like a power struggle, an attempt to assert dominance in a situation where he felt threatened, even though there was no real threat. He couldn't handle the idea that someone else, even a woman, could shift the attention away from him for a brief moment. His outburst wasn't about love or protectiveness but his need to maintain control over me and the situation.

He would call me late at night, around 10 or 11 PM, asking me to come over, saying things like, "I miss you; I just want to hold you." At the time, I didn't see it for what it was. I was already in bed most nights, but he would pick a fight over the phone or through texts every time he wasn't with me. It became a pattern, something I now refer to as his "four days on, three days off" cycle. This cycle seemed more prominent in Florida as our time together followed a routine. Thursday through Sunday, we would go out, brunch on Sundays, and spend time together. Those were his "good" days when he was on his best behavior.

However, he would become mean, distant, and angry Sunday night through Wednesday, mostly through texts. I never understood why he picked fights when he wasn't even with me. It made no sense then, but now I see it was part of his control cycle. He created chaos even from afar. His behavior was erratic, and I often wondered what I had done wrong. Anytime he was drinking or angry, especially when we were at my house in Florida, the verbal abuse would escalate. He would hurl insults, calling me names like "bitch" or worse. There was a pattern of him picking fights to get out of spending the night after I had already said yes. It was as if he thrived on the chaos he caused.

The emotional exhaustion from his constant manipulation was overwhelming. He was always creating confusion and chaos, so I couldn't see what was happening before me. I was too caught up in trying to keep the peace, and I didn't realize I was being controlled. The physical aspect of his abuse started in Florida as well. When his verbal tirades weren't enough, there were a few occasions where he became physically aggressive. I remember slapping him across the face once when he wouldn't stop. His response was terrifying—he threw me on the bed, using his full weight to pin me down. He was far from small at six foot four and over 200 pounds. I cried and begged him to get off, telling him I couldn't breathe. He knew exactly what he was doing. I shared with him that my son's biological father had choked me in the past, and he used that vulnerability against me.

His abuse wasn't limited to just verbal or physical attacks. He took everything I had ever confided in him and turned it into a weapon. He knew I hated feeling smothered, and he tried to exploit that fear in his way. The psychological toll of his behavior was just as damaging as the physical acts. He was using my past traumas to trigger new ones, forcing me to relive experiences I had spent years trying to move past. It was a twisted game of control that left me gasping for air in more ways than one. The physical abuse worsened when we moved to my house in South Dakota in May 2023. The isolation of living in a rural area gave him more freedom to act out. He knew there was no one nearby who could hear me or intervene.

In South Dakota, his behavior escalated. He would grab me, shove me, throw me up against walls, and push me around the house. I was out in the middle of nowhere, and he knew it. There was no one to witness the abuse or come to my aid. His psychological abuse worsened, too. He made passive-aggressive comments about my past, knowing full well the pain they caused. He would say things like, "I just want to rape you," in a way that was both cruel and degrading. It wasn't just a careless comment but a deliberate attempt to provoke and hurt me.

He would try to push me into reacting, sometimes wanting me to hit him, as if that would justify his actions. He was a sadist in every sense, and even my lawyer later confirmed it. Things became so unbearable by August that he finally left. The months following his departure were a blur of physical and emotional devastation. In just a few short months, I lost significant weight. It wasn't because I wasn't eating—I was, though not as much as usual. It was the trauma that consumed me. I spent the first week after he left barely existing, sitting on the couch, crying uncontrollably. My son was there, thank God, because I'm not sure I would've made it through those days alone.

I had responsibilities—a full garden to tend to, chickens, ducks, and turkeys to care for—but I was barely functioning. I would find myself out in the garden, tears streaming down my face, unable to comprehend why I felt so lost. He hadn't just left; he had left with a new supply, someone else to manipulate. Narcissists never leave without someone waiting in the wings. That realization was another layer of betrayal I had to deal with. He hadn't just discarded me; he had moved on to his next victim, leaving me shattered in the aftermath.

To this day, Andrew continues to lie about leaving me for someone else despite all the signs pointing to it. He insists it's not true, but just because I don't have physical proof doesn't mean it didn't happen. His defensiveness and anger whenever the topic came up were clear indicators. Narcissists like him tend to project their behavior onto others. In my case, he constantly accused me of cheating or lying, even when I was doing something as innocent as visiting my husband in memory care. One time, when I told him I was heading to see Dan, Andrew immediately accused me of lying and cheating, launching into a three-day-long rant about my supposed infidelity. He had me so confused and mentally exhausted that I took photos of my surroundings to prove my innocence. Looking back, it seems absurd, but his constant accusations wore me down at the time.

The emotional toll of constantly defending myself from his baseless accusations was exhausting. My relationship with my husband had been passive-aggressive and covert in many ways, but Andrew was a different type of manipulator. He was more overt and volatile, though he also had a covert side that made his manipulation even more insidious. My son was the first to point out that Andrew was a narcissist. He had dated someone with similar traits and recognized the same patterns in Andrew's behavior. It wasn't until then that I started researching narcissism, and it all clicked. The constant accusations, gaslighting, and manipulation all made sense. But even with this newfound understanding, I didn't learn my lesson right away.

In November of last year, I mistakenly asked Andrew to accompany me on a trip to Colorado to pick up my horse. The drive back was a nightmare. At some point during the drive, he started raging about something trivial, and it quickly escalated. We were in the middle of nowhere, driving through Nebraska during the winter after a snowstorm. All around us were endless fields, and I had no cell service. He threatened to stop the truck, get out, and take the keys, leaving me stranded with a horse in a trailer and my small dog. He stopped the truck twice or thrice, each time making the same threat. I was terrified he would leave me alone in the freezing cold with no way to get home. I had to soothe him, pretending to be calm and agreeable, to ensure we returned safely.

That trip was just one example of the many insane situations I encountered because of Andrew. Even after everything, I still didn't fully distance myself. When my son's horse was injured in December, I asked Andrew to come and stay with me for a couple of months to help out. I realized how foolish I was. Within a few weeks of him returning to my house, I couldn't stand him anymore. His presence, his constant negativity, and the never-ending fights were unbearable. I ended up paying him to stay at an Airbnb to get him out of my house. I didn't want him there anymore. Eventually, he moved into his place in the next town over, but the turmoil didn't stop. The fights, the emotional manipulation—it all continued, and I found myself caught in a cycle of chaos that I couldn't seem to break free from.

The constant gaslighting made me doubt my reality. He would tell me we weren't even together, despite spending almost every weekend with me, or accuse me of things I hadn't done. I would find myself questioning my memory, actions, and sanity. It was a slow, insidious process, but over time, his manipulation had me tied up in knots, unsure of what was real and what wasn't. Every argument and accusation was designed to keep me off balance, maintain control over me, and ensure I was constantly seeking his approval or validation.

In April, everything escalated to the point where Andrew got me arrested for defending myself. He had dropped off a load of supplies for me, including a bag of animal feed. When I pointed out that one of the bags had a hole in it and told him he needed to take it back, he immediately lost it. I reminded him that he had purchased it with his card a few weeks ago, and although I had paid him back in cash, I didn't have the receipt to handle the return, so he would need to take care of it. That simple request was enough to send him into a fit of rage. He started screaming at me, yelling that the store wouldn't take it back, and his anger only intensified.

I had recently broken four ribs at the end of February in a fall while mounting my horse without a saddle. I was still recovering, unsure if my ribs had fully healed, and here I was, trying to stay calm while Andrew was out of control. He was furious, yelling and raging. As he got more aggressive, he started aggressing towards me with his chest and slamming me against his truck. I was scared and unsure if my body could handle the impact. In a desperate attempt to stop the situation from escalating, I sat inside his truck to keep him from pushing me against it.

But that didn't stop him. He began pulling on my legs, trying to drag me out of the truck. I quickly closed the door to prevent him from physically pulling me out. People often ask, "Why didn't you just call 911?" Sitting in the barn, my phone was about 20 feet away, but more than that, I was scared. People don't realize how terrifying it is to be in that moment, with someone bigger and stronger screaming at you and losing control. I froze, unsure of what to do. It's easy to say what you would have done when you're not in the situation, but fear takes over when you're in it.

At this point, I had my utility knife in my front pocket, and it was digging into my leg while I was sitting in the truck. I took it out, but I didn't intend to use it. It was just uncomfortable. He saw me holding the knife and started taunting me, yelling, "What are you gonna do?" He kept advancing toward me, backing me up against the truck again, and I was terrified. I told him, "You need to get the fuck away from me," but he didn't stop. He kept coming, screaming in my face. In self-defense, I used the knife. I didn't want to, but he left me no choice. I didn't stab him deeply—it was just a small poke in the shoulder. He didn't even go to the hospital, and the cut was tiny, but he acted like I had severely injured him.

He called 911, trying to paint me as the aggressor. At the time, I didn't realize why he called the police so quickly, but later, I found out he saw me on my phone and thought I was calling the cops. He was trying to get ahead of the situation, fearing that I would claim self-defense, which is exactly what it was. But at that moment, I wasn't calling 911. I was on the phone with my son, telling him what had happened. My son told me I needed to call the police immediately, so I did.

That night was a turning point. Andrew hung his head as the reality of the situation hit him. I got a no-contact order, but it could have been much worse. I was facing the possibility of being charged with a felony. That thought still haunts me. He kept texting me after the incident, trying to bait me into responding. If I had replied, I would have violated the no-contact order, which could have led to serious legal trouble. Thankfully, I didn't fall into his trap. My lawyer advised me to forward everything to her, which I did. I even unblocked him on social media for a day to see what he was doing. Immediately, he started watching my Instagram stories, but I screenshot everything and then blocked him again.

What Andrew didn't know was that I had pictures of my back, which was covered in bruises from when he had slammed me against the truck. Those photos were my evidence of his abuse. Despite everything, he manipulated the situation to make me look like the villain. It was just like every other time—he played the victim while I was left to deal with the physical and emotional damage.

I had never been to jail before. I had never experienced anything even close to it. So, when I found myself spending a night in jail, it felt like my entire world had been flipped upside down. I thought I was going to die. Looking back,

I'm thankful it happened in South Dakota because it could have been much worse. The jail I was in was more of a holding facility, and while it wasn't as bad as what I'd imagine in a bigger state like New York, it was still terrible for me. By the time they processed me and I was placed in my cell, it was close to midnight. The next morning, around six or seven, they opened the doors to a large community room with tables where you could make phone calls if needed. It wasn't the nightmare I'd always imagined but still a nightmare for me.

I was on the phone with my son, crying and feeling helpless. All I could think about was my horses. Who was going to take care of them? They meant the world to me, and I didn't have anyone to handle them. Ultimately, the only person my son could reach at that late hour was the guy who remodeled our house. He lived one town over and knew nothing about horses. Horses can be stubborn, especially when handled by someone unfamiliar, and this man struggled to get them into the barn, none of which was his fault and I was grateful that he went and did this for me. It broke my heart knowing my animals were stressed and out of their routine because of everything happening to me. The trauma of that night extended beyond me; it affected them, too.

It took me nearly a month—maybe even longer—to get the horses comfortable enough to return to the barn without a struggle. Every night became a battle, with me spending at least an hour coaxing them in. It reminded me that Andrew's actions didn't just impact me—they disrupted everything around me, including my animals. The devastation was overwhelming. I couldn't believe that this was how things ended after everything I had done for him. He knew exactly how much my animals meant to me, and I do not doubt that he was happy knowing they were affected, too. That's the cruelty of someone like him—they know exactly where to strike to hurt you the most. Andrew's ability to use my love for my animals as a weapon against me perfectly illustrates this tactic of intentional cruelty.

In the aftermath of that night, I struggled with how this experience had changed me. I found myself questioning whether I could ever trust or date someone again. How does one move forward after being betrayed and hurt so deeply? It makes you wonder if there are genuinely decent people out there. I'm sure there are, but after everything I've been through, it's hard to imagine finding someone I could trust. Some days, I'm fine, but then something triggers me, and the emotions come flooding back—anger, sadness, frustration. The hardest part is trying to understand why. Why did he do this to me? Why, after everything I gave and sacrificed, was I left with nothing but pain?

The deep dive I've taken into understanding narcissism has been the only thing that's helped me make sense of it. Learning about how they operate, how they manipulate, and why they behave the way they do has been eye-opening. It wasn't about me, even though he tried to make me think it was. He always blamed me, saying it was how I talked to him or the tone of my voice. He spent months last summer telling me I was the problem. But I started questioning it. I asked my son, who is brutally honest with me, if he thought I was being unreasonable or if I had a tone when I talked. My son is the type to call me out if I'm wrong, but he even told me that Andrew was the issue.

My son had his own experience with a narcissist, and we both went through it last summer. We called it the "narcissist summer." We were both dealing with the aftermath of toxic relationships, both getting texts from our exes and both feeling the frustration and anger that comes with trying to break free from someone who won't let you go. During the day, we'd handle the work that needed to be done around the farm, but by night, we were looking for distractions. We'd say we weren't going to go out, but by five o'clock, one of us would text the other, and off we'd go—drinking, gambling, trying to numb the pain. It became a cycle of avoiding our feelings and diving into temporary escapes, only to have everything crash down on us again.

We'd go out to the big casino, have drinks, dance, go to concerts—anything to drown out the emotions we didn't want to face. But no matter how much fun we had, the reality of what we had both been through hit us hard. The pain, the betrayal, the emotional scars—they didn't go away just because we tried to ignore them. If anything, our attempts to escape only delayed the inevitable emotional crash. The more we tried to avoid it, the harder it hit when the distractions weren't enough anymore.

That summer of trying to escape was, in a way, part of the healing process. We had to get it out of our system before facing the reality of what we had endured. The emotional scars Andrew left on me are still there. As the old proverb says, *"The axe forgets, but the tree remembers."* It's not something that goes away overnight; there are still days when I feel like I'm drowning in the aftermath. But through all of it, I'm learning how to rebuild. Understanding that it wasn't my fault, that his actions reflected his issues and not my worth, has been crucial in moving forward.

Chapter 11: Rock Bottom: The Arrest and Its Aftermath

The legal process I endured was stressful and confusing, marked by varying emotions. It all started with a preliminary hearing, the first and only legal proceeding I attended. After that, Andrew refused to cooperate with the authorities. I can only speculate about his reasons for this decision. Maybe he didn't want to see me go to jail or feared that if the process continued, his behavior would come under scrutiny. My suspicion leans toward the latter but without clear evidence.

The most frustrating aspect of this entire ordeal was trying to explain Andrew's behavior to my lawyer. Andrew's behavior was inconsistent and deceitful. I felt a deep sense of frustration trying to make my lawyer understand this side of him, as narcissistic behavior isn't something easily understood by those who haven't personally experienced it. It reminded me of the struggle often described in *The Gift of Fear* by Gavin de Becker, where victims of manipulation have to rely on their instincts while those around them may not fully comprehend the emotional and psychological toll of the situation. Despite these challenges, my lawyer remained focused on the technicalities of the case, and I had to follow along with her guidance.

Throughout this process, I was dealing with the possibility that Andrew might try to sabotage me in some way before the dismissal date. He had already caused enough problems for me, and I knew his behavior could escalate. My instinct told me he might try to stir up more trouble as the court date drew near, which added an overwhelming amount of anxiety. I kept telling my lawyer that we needed to push for the dismissal before that date to avoid any additional conflict. Fortunately, we were able to get the dismissal granted ahead of time, which relieved a great deal of stress.

One thing that worked in my favor was Andrew's inconsistency. Narcissists, by nature, often end up exposing themselves through their erratic behavior, and Andrew was no exception. His inability to maintain a coherent narrative or stick to a consistent course of action made it easier for my lawyer to build a case against him. His contradictory actions—such as following me on social media, sending confusing and sometimes threatening text messages, and attempting to reestablish contact—created a clear pattern of instability. It was as if he couldn't help but leave behind a trail of evidence. His efforts to manipulate the situation only backfired, exposing his true nature.

Whenever he did something irrational or impulsive, my lawyer would immediately document the behavior and inform the state's attorney. This helped demonstrate Andrew's lack of credibility, showing that his claims were unreliable. In a way, Andrew's actions were working against him, building the case for my defense without any need for me to say much. Each time he acted out of line, he provided more proof that his intentions were malicious and not rooted in truth. My lawyer used every one of these moments to strengthen the argument that I was the victim of his abuse and manipulation rather than the perpetrator.

Still, the legal process was not without its challenges for me; it felt like walking through a storm, with obstacles at every turn and no clear path to calm. I had to agree to see a therapist, who would write a letter confirming that I was mentally stable. Although this requirement felt unnecessary, I complied because it was a small step toward securing the dismissal. Once that hurdle was crossed, my lawyer kept reminding me that my clean record would work in my favor. I didn't have any previous legal issues—no criminal history, no traffic violations. In contrast, Andrew had a past that included a DWI felony. His track record made him look far from credible, especially when compared to mine.

Despite my lawyer's reassurance, the fear and mental strain of the process weighed heavily on me. I kept imagining worst-case scenarios where Andrew might try to frame me or worsen the situation as the court date approached. My mind was constantly racing with thoughts of how he could manipulate the situation, but in the end, his actions turned out to be his undoing. As the old saying goes, *"The wheels of justice turn slowly but grind exceedingly fine."* Andrew's behavior, in the end, was the very thing that allowed me to secure the dismissal.

The dismissal of the charges against me came just in time, about a week or week and a half before the court date. This early dismissal brought relief, but it also triggered anger and frustration from Andrew, who had instigated the entire legal situation. After the dismissal, he immediately deleted his Instagram account, only to create a new one and start following me again. His erratic behavior was confusing and unsettling, yet it was a pattern that had become all too familiar. While I was happy the case had been resolved in my favor, the tension from dealing with his unpredictable actions still weighed heavily on me.

During this period, my lawyer sent Andrew a no-trespass letter, ensuring he couldn't come near my home or approach me in any way. This letter was a protective barrier; if he violated it, I could call the authorities, and he would be arrested. Despite having this legal protection, the stress of the entire situation remained. I felt angry and infuriated because, from the start, I knew I shouldn't have been arrested. It was an unjust situation that never should have escalated to this level. The legal process added to my anxiety, making it a deeply exhausting experience.

A large part of the stress stemmed from the fear of retaliation. I constantly worried about what Andrew might do next. His unpredictable behavior had me contemplating extreme measures to protect myself. For a while, I was convinced I needed to move far away, possibly to Colorado. I considered changing my phone number and even changing my name to ensure he couldn't track me down. This desire to flee and disappear is common among survivors of narcissistic abuse, as the psychological impact of the manipulation and control often makes them feel unsafe, even when physical danger may not be present. It's a mental and emotional exhaustion that leaves you wanting to escape completely.

The emotional toll of psychological abuse is immense. I sometimes wanted to be in a witness protection program where I could entirely vanish from Andrew's radar. His manipulation had such an effect on me that it seemed like the only way to regain control of my life was to disappear. However, over time, I began working through these emotions. I had a strong support system and an energy worker who helped me through somatic healing techniques. These practices helped me regain my sense of safety and reduced the feeling that Andrew had no power over me.

Eventually, I realized that I didn't need to run away. I decided to stay and build my horse farm, which gave me a sense of stability and control. While I can't predict the future or say with absolute certainty that I'll stay forever, for now, I'm committed to creating a life that feels secure. The legal protections, such as the no-trespass order and emotional work I've done, have allowed me to rebuild my confidence and sense of safety.

The dismissal meant that I was forced into a period of no contact with Andrew, and it was during this time that I began to break free from the trauma bond that had kept me tethered to him emotionally. Narcissistic abuse survivors often struggle to break these bonds because the manipulation creates a sense of hopelessness and confusion, where the victim feels stuck and unable to function. But as time passed,

I found that the distance helped me recover from the psychological hold Andrew had over me.

By the time I received the dismissal, nearly 90 days had passed since the legal process began. This extended period of no contact was vital in helping me heal. Breaking the trauma bond wasn't easy, but once I got past a certain point, I began to feel more empowered. I was no longer frozen in a state of fear or anxiety, and I started to reclaim my ability to make decisions and move forward in my life. The dismissal wasn't just the end of a legal case; it was the beginning of my emotional recovery.

Chapter 12: The Journey Inward: Seeking Professional Help

I have always sought help from healing modalities because of the challenges and emotional turmoil I've faced throughout my life. These challenges created emotional scars that I struggled to manage on my own, pushing me to seek guidance from those who could offer clarity and relief. Working with a spiritual mentor became a vital part of this journey. In 2022, I connected with my current mentor, whose wisdom and approach to healing aligned with my need for deeper understanding and peace. The mentor's guidance allowed me to reflect on my inner struggles and work through the overwhelming feelings that had accumulated over the years. Choosing this path was not just about seeking advice but also about having someone who could help me explore the deeper layers of emotional and spiritual well-being.

In addition to spiritual mentorship, I sought help from an energy worker to bring balance and alignment to my emotional state. By the middle of 2022, I felt that the emotional baggage I had been carrying was holding me back from fully embracing life and achieving inner calm. My energy worker played an important role in helping me understand how external forces, such as past relationships and unresolved emotions, were affecting my mental and physical health. Her sessions allowed me to release built-up negativity and regain control over my emotional state. This wasn't just about feeling better temporarily; it was about creating a lasting shift in how I approached healing and self-care. The decision to work with her came naturally, as I knew I needed to take control of my well-being in a way that addressed not only the surface-level issues but also the deeper emotional imbalances.

Choosing to work with these two healing modalities—spiritual mentorship and energy work—was a turning point in my journey toward self-awareness and emotional recovery. Each provided a unique approach that catered to different aspects of my healing process. My spiritual mentor helped me address the underlying emotional and spiritual conflicts, while my energy worker guided me through releasing the emotional burdens I had accumulated. Together, their support empowered me to face life's difficulties with a sense of calm and balance that I hadn't experienced before. Both relationships were integral in helping me regain control of my mental and emotional state, allowing me to process the challenges in my life more effectively. Without their guidance, I would not have been able to navigate through some of the most difficult periods of my life with the strength and resilience I eventually discovered.

However, by 2023, life became increasingly chaotic, especially due to my relationship with Andrew. The constant stress and unpredictability in our relationship began to consume much of my time and energy. I found myself pulling away from the very practices that had once been my lifeline, helping me maintain my emotional and spiritual well-being. These sessions, which had been essential in grounding me, started to feel like something I could no longer fit into my increasingly hectic schedule. I slowly reduced my meetings with both my spiritual mentor and energy worker, not because I wanted to, but because I felt drained by the constant demands on my attention and energy. This withdrawal from my healing routine left me feeling more lost and disconnected from myself, adding to the growing sense of chaos in my life.

One of the major reasons I stopped engaging with my mentors regularly was Andrew's behavior. His actions seemed to deliberately create obstacles that made it hard for me to find the privacy I needed for my sessions. He would complain about the time I spent away from him, even if it was just a brief session, and his objections became a constant source of tension. This behavior mirrored that of my late husband, Dan, who had also found ways to subtly interfere with my personal growth by making it difficult for me to carve out time for myself. Over time, this pattern of behavior from both men became more apparent, and it was something I had to face head-on. The need for privacy during these healing sessions, something both Dan and Andrew seemed to resent, highlighted how deeply their actions affected my ability to prioritize my emotional health.

The physical environment I was living in at the time also contributed to my decision to pause my healing sessions. My house in South Dakota was much smaller than my previous homes, making it increasingly difficult to find a quiet and private space to meet with my spiritual mentor or energy worker. In my previous homes, I could easily shut my bedroom door and create a peaceful space for these meetings, but in South Dakota, the layout of the house didn't offer the same level of privacy. My bedroom was close to the kitchen, and the lack of distance made it impossible to have uninterrupted, focused sessions. This discomfort increased my frustration, making it harder to engage in the practices that had once brought me so much comfort and clarity.

The combination of Andrew's behavior and the limitations of my physical space left me feeling trapped and disconnected from the very tools that had always helped me maintain balance. Andrew's controlling nature, coupled with the confined physical environment, triggered a sense of powerlessness. This situation aligns with a psychological phenomenon called learned helplessness, where repeated exposure to stressful or uncontrollable circumstances causes a person to feel like they have no agency over their situation. As Andrew made it increasingly difficult for me to find time and space for myself, I began to withdraw, feeling as though my efforts to regain balance were futile. This emotional withdrawal led me to stop reaching out for the support I knew I needed from my spiritual mentor and energy worker, leaving me in a state of emotional isolation.

The more I distanced myself from my spiritual practices, the more overwhelming the sense of disarray in my life became. It wasn't just about the loss of routine; it was the deep sense of losing touch with the part of myself that had always sought growth and healing. The absence of these practices not only deprived me of my emotional outlets but also disconnected me from my sense of identity. According to psychological theories on self-concept, when we are cut off from activities and practices that contribute to our personal growth, we can experience a fragmentation of our identity. For me, spiritual mentorship and energy work were vital to my sense of self, and as those practices faded from my life, so did my sense of personal empowerment and emotional stability.

As time passed, I realized how much I had put my healing journey on hold due to the overwhelming external factors in my life. After Andrew left, I didn't immediately return to working with my spiritual mentor or energy worker because I needed time to process the emotional weight of everything that had transpired. I felt disconnected from myself, and before I could reengage with my healing practices, I needed to regain my sense of identity outside of that turbulent relationship. The process of reflection and self-assessment took longer than I had anticipated, but I knew it was necessary. Eventually, after my son had left, I finally had the space and quiet to focus on my well-being again.

Once I resumed my sessions with my spiritual mentor, I felt a sense of relief. It was as if I had been carrying an invisible burden that I could now finally set down. As the meetings became more frequent, I quickly realized how much I had missed that connection and the clarity it brought to my life. The lingering energy from my past relationships, especially with Andrew, had continued to affect me long after his departure. His emotional presence felt like a shadow, influencing my thoughts and feelings. As Maya Angelou once said, *"You can't really know where you are going until you know where you have been."* I knew I needed to clear that energy to move forward. My spiritual mentor guided me through this process, helping me address the unresolved emotions and face the complex feelings that had built up. Through their support, I could release the past and begin healing.

Throughout my healing journey, I've understood that I didn't always have proper, energetic boundaries in place. When I began working with my spiritual mentor and energy worker, I was already seeking support, but I hadn't fully grasped how to protect my energy. I also worked with a narcissistic abuse recovery coach for about four weeks. To be honest, I now realize that there are probably better coaches out there. After gaining more knowledge, it became clear to me that many so-called experts in this field lack a true understanding of what they're doing. For a while, I even questioned whether the coach I worked with truly had the qualifications needed to support people like me who were dealing with the aftermath of narcissistic abuse.

At one point, I began doubting the intentions of the coach. It seemed like he was more focused on benefiting from my efforts rather than genuinely helping me heal. I had already considered hosting retreats or workshops, though I wasn't planning on becoming a coach. Out of nowhere, this coach suggested we collaborate on a retreat together. However, as the conversation unfolded, it became apparent that his interest was primarily in having me handle all the work while he leveraged his large following to claim credit. This made me realize that his behavior was, in itself, narcissistic. I thought to myself, "I don't need this." I didn't care about having a big following then; I knew I could build one on my own if needed. It became clear that working with this coach wasn't in my best interest, so I cut ties with him and moved on.

Looking back on this experience, I often consider the large number of individuals who present themselves as coaches or experts in narcissistic abuse recovery. While some may have gone through similar situations, that alone doesn't automatically qualify them to guide others through the healing process. Many of these self-proclaimed experts haven't taken the time to do thorough research or educate themselves on the psychological terminology that's vital for understanding the true dynamics of abuse. This lack of knowledge leads to the spread of misinformation, which can harm those who are already vulnerable and seeking help.

A prime example of this misunderstanding is the term "reactive abuse." I've seen many coaches teach that reactive abuse occurs when the victim reacts to the abuse and somehow becomes the abuser. This is completely incorrect. In reality, reactive abuse refers to the abuser intentionally provoking a reaction from the victim, and that act of provocation is the abuse itself. I frequently encounter people who feel confused and anxious, wondering if they are the abuser simply because they reacted. I have to explain to them that their reaction is not abusive and help them understand what reactive abuse truly is. The widespread misinformation surrounding these terms is deeply concerning, and it frustrates me to see how many people are being led astray. Books like *Healing from Hidden Abuse* by Shannon Thomas offer a clear explanation of concepts like reactive abuse, helping victims understand how abusers manipulate situations to make them feel guilty for their reactions.

Choosing the right modalities for healing became even more crucial to me after my experiences with these so-called "coaches." Having worked as an art therapist, I understood that traditional talk therapy wasn't enough. I had attended therapy sessions in my younger years, but they never seemed to bring the deep healing I was looking for. Talk therapy often keeps people stuck in a loop, focusing on what's wrong without offering practical solutions to move forward. It rarely addresses how to process trauma through the body or stop ruminating thoughts. I knew that if I wanted to truly heal, I needed something beyond talking about my problems. I needed methods that could help me shift out of the pain and trauma, not just keep me focused on them.

In my healing process, I had to explore different methods and be willing to experiment. I became my test subject, trying out various approaches to see what worked. This wasn't just for my healing but also because I wanted to make sure that any advice I gave to others would be effective. It wasn't enough to follow the advice of someone who simply said, "Healing takes time." I wasn't interested in staying stuck for years, waiting for things to get better on their own. I knew that with enough determination, I could accelerate the process. This mindset drove me to explore deeper healing modalities, methods that would not only help me but also allow me to share valuable insights with others on their healing journeys.

I've realized the power of shifting our mindset through some of the profound messages shared by a spiritual influencer named Brashar, whom I follow on Instagram and TikTok. His content has greatly impacted me, particularly how he talks about how healing doesn't have to take forever. He explains it very simply: "*If you want to believe that it's going to take all this time to heal and you want to prolong your suffering, then by all means, I'm not going to stop you, but you can just stop.*" This idea was eye-opening for me. It made me reflect on how much of my healing journey was influenced by the belief that it had to be a slow, painful process. The realization that I could make a conscious decision to let go of the suffering and move forward was transformative.

As strange as it sounds, it's true—mind over matter. The idea that we can choose to stop feeling terrible and start living better is incredibly powerful. Brashar's message showed me that healing isn't always about how much time has passed but rather about deciding to change. It's about breaking free from the belief that healing must be a slow, painful journey filled with endless emotional struggles. Instead, we can take control by consciously deciding to focus on the present moment and embrace feeling better. This approach means letting go of the idea that pain and suffering are necessary for growth and, instead, recognizing that healing can happen when we allow ourselves to feel joy and peace.

What I love about Brashar's approach is that he encourages people to let go of limiting beliefs. He explains that we often hold ourselves back because our minds only imagine what we think is possible. He challenges people to think big and get excited about their goals but then to drop those thoughts and let the universe work out the details. He says our imaginations are limited, so if we let go of what we think is possible, we allow the universe to bring us something even better. This idea really struck me. For example, I was thinking about how I wanted to help people heal faster through my book and online classes. I had this plan in my head, and it was good but not groundbreaking. Then something unexpected happened—James reached out to me about doing a TV interview. Suddenly, the possibility of reaching a much larger audience opened up. I realized that by letting go of what I thought my plan should be, something much bigger and better came into my life.

This idea of allowing life to be easier and letting go of struggles really started to change my perspective. My energy worker also pointed out that perhaps I had spent previous lifetimes learning things the hard way, but I didn't have to do that anymore. She encouraged me to choose an easier path, and that's been my focus lately. I'm done with unnecessary hardships and feeling stuck. I'm letting go of all the negativity and embracing a smoother, more fulfilling journey. Eclipse season has been the perfect time for this transformation. I've been working closely with my spiritual mentor, who has helped me understand my astrological chart and how things like Neptune's influence have played a role in my life. Though I don't always fully grasp the specifics of astrology, I trust the guidance I've been receiving. These insights have given me more clarity on how to align with the changes I'm experiencing.

Astrology has played a fascinating role in my healing as well. I've been receiving readings from Kasia, who doesn't just focus on astrology but also incorporates tarot into her readings. She emphasizes that emotions are something we can feel without becoming them. This idea of observing emotions and letting them pass, rather than letting them define us, has been key in my healing. I've noticed that in the past few months, whenever I find myself overthinking or getting caught up in emotions, I now have tools to manage them. It's often when I'm doing something mindless, like cleaning the horse stalls, that my mind starts to wander. But instead of spiraling, I now recognize those thoughts and let them pass. It's been a game changer for my emotional well-being.

The teachings I've been following have reinforced the importance of mental discipline. In one of my recent sessions with my spiritual mentor, we discussed the power of belief and how it shapes our reality. It reminded me of a book I've been reading, *You Are the Placebo*, by Dr. Joe Dispenza. The book explores the concept that we can change our physical and emotional state simply by shifting our beliefs. Dr. Dispenza provides scientific evidence of how people have healed from serious illnesses just by altering their mindset. This aligns perfectly with what I've learned from Brashar—that if we truly believe that we can heal quickly, we will. It's about breaking free from limiting thoughts and opening ourselves to the possibility that life doesn't have to be a constant struggle.

One of the most significant breakthroughs I've had came when I decided to embrace this new way of thinking. I realized that I don't have the emotional baggage from previous relationships. I can choose to let it go and focus on what I want my life to look like moving forward. It's been empowering to recognize that I'm not stuck in a cycle of endless healing or hardship. By changing my mindset, I've started to see changes in my external reality as well. Opportunities are coming my way, and life feels lighter and more enjoyable. This shift in perspective has been one of the most liberating experiences of my life.

I've also noticed that as I've embraced this mindset, my ability to manage day-to-day challenges has improved. I no longer feel overwhelmed by small setbacks or difficulties. Instead, I approach them with a sense of curiosity and openness, knowing that they are temporary and that I have the power to shift my focus. This has been especially helpful when it comes to dealing with financial stress or other practical concerns. As Brashar said, *"If you don't want to struggle financially, you just decide not to."* It's not about ignoring reality but rather changing how you respond to it. This mindset shift has allowed me to approach my finances and other areas of life with more ease and less fear.

Over time, I've come to understand that emotions, like sadness, are meant to pass through us, not stay stuck. Nowadays, when I feel sad or overwhelmed, I let myself cry for a moment, but then I remind myself that I don't have to hold on to that sadness. It doesn't define me or my day. It's just energy moving through me. I've learned to let those feelings come and go without attaching myself to them. This shift in thinking has changed how I handle difficult emotions. Instead of holding onto them or letting them ruin my day, I acknowledge them and let them pass as they're meant to. We, as humans, often get stuck by attaching ourselves to things like past experiences or painful memories, thinking they define us.

A big part of this process is realizing how much we cling to our old stories. Whether it's something from childhood or a past relationship, we sometimes believe that our future has to mirror those experiences. This keeps us stuck. We tell ourselves, "My life is this way because of my past," and in doing so, we limit our ability to grow. But we don't have to remain small because of what we've been through. Our history will always be a part of us, but we don't need to let it dictate our present. When we live fully in the present, we can make different choices, experience more freedom, and see new possibilities. The past only holds us back if we allow it to.

This realization extends even to something as simple as time. I used to stress out constantly about not having enough time. There was always a sense of urgency, this feeling that I needed to rush through my tasks because there wasn't enough time to do it all. But the moment I let go of that mindset, everything started falling into place. I found that I did have time for everything, and things started happening more smoothly. For instance, I would be cleaning the horse stalls and thinking, "I've only got an hour to get all of this done." But somehow, it always got done, and I realized that I was the one creating the stress. Once I stopped worrying about time and started trusting that things would work out, they did.

I've come to understand that the pressure I used to put on myself to get everything done perfectly and on time was rooted in something much deeper. Growing up in a narcissistic household and later being married to a narcissist conditioned me to believe that my worth was tied to how much I accomplished. With my mom and my husband, I was always the one doing the work. Narcissists often convince you that you're the one who has to handle everything in order to keep life moving smoothly. My husband, for example, would come home, and if I wasn't working or hadn't been busy enough, he would make passive-aggressive comments.

It took me a long time to realize that I didn't have to live like that anymore.

I've now come to embrace the idea that I can take breaks, do things I enjoy, and not feel guilty. I've learned that I don't have to be constantly working to be valuable. If I want to ride my horse before doing any work, I can do that. No one owns my time except me, and I've had to retrain my mind to accept that. As the saying goes, *"Rest is not a reward for hard work; it is a necessary part of it."* For so long, I lived in a dynamic where I felt like I had to earn the right to relax or enjoy life. Now, I see that rest and enjoyment are essential to my well-being, not something I need to justify. Breaking free from that mindset has been a journey, but it's one of the most liberating things I've done for myself.

A funny realization hit me recently when I was talking to my son. We were discussing narcissists and how they function, and I suddenly realized just how emotionally stunted many narcissists are. They often talk about their intelligence or capability, but in reality, they struggle with even basic emotional growth. Looking back at my experiences, especially with my husband, I noticed how immature his behavior truly was. For example, he would talk about how he could fix things around the house, but he never actually did it. Despite having a successful business, he never applied that same work ethic at home, and I was left doing everything.

This dynamic of narcissists pushing all the responsibility onto others became so clear to me once I stepped away from it. I now understand how much I was carrying and how little they actually did. And this pattern isn't unique to me—many people who've dealt with narcissists in their lives share similar stories. These individuals create an illusion of being capable, but they rarely follow through on their responsibilities. It's like they remain emotionally stuck, never truly growing beyond a certain point, which leaves their partners or family members picking up the slack. I realized that this behavior drains those around them, both emotionally and physically. The constant burden can lead to stress and burnout for the ones who are left to manage everything.

It became clear to me why things worked the way they did. My husband, Dan, didn't actually do much in terms of running his business. He relied heavily on the people working for him, including myself. When I first met him, he hired me to work for his business, so I was working for him before we actually got together. As I started helping out, it quickly became evident that he didn't handle the actual work; he mostly attended meetings and made it seem like he knew what he was doing. He had a charismatic way of talking, which is something many narcissists use to their advantage. They're good at giving the appearance of competence, saying the right things in meetings, and making people believe they are in control. But the reality was the office staff and the people in the field were doing the work.

When I began working for him, I gradually started taking over more responsibilities. I didn't just help out with minor tasks; I took on accounting and eventually moved into project management. I was invested in the success of the company as if it were my own, and I was the reason we made so much money during that time. The more I contributed, the more successful the business became. But what was he doing? Not much, except showing up to meetings and acting like the mastermind behind it all. He didn't need to understand the details or manage the projects himself because I, along with the people who worked for him, was handling it all. I was initially hired as the accountant but took on more roles as the business grew, eventually running the office. Later, when he downsized the business and many employees either left or were let go, I began managing many of the projects from inside the office.

I've always been good at business because I grew up in it. I understood how to make things run smoothly, and I knew how to handle finances. Dan benefitted greatly from that. In a way, I was his secret weapon, and it's no wonder he didn't want to let me go. For a narcissist, having someone like me around was like hitting the jackpot. Not only was I making the business successful, but I was also doing it all while giving him the spotlight. He loved money, and I was helping him make more of it than he could have on his own. Narcissists are greedy by nature, and my contributions were exactly what he needed to keep feeding that greed.

It's mind-blowing when you step back and see how narcissists, who pride themselves on being so intelligent and capable, are actually completely reliant on the people around them. He was no different. He acted like he was the mastermind, but in reality, I was the one behind the scenes doing all the real work. The people who worked for him and I were the ones making sure everything got done while he took the credit. My son and I found it both funny and frustrating when looking back on all the effort I put in, while he basked in the glory without lifting a finger.

This understanding has a freeing effect in many ways. Narcissists operate under the illusion that they're the ones in control, but the truth is they depend on others to do the heavy lifting. They live in a bubble of their own creation, where they manipulate others into doing the work and maintaining the appearance that they are the ones running the show. It wasn't until I finally stepped away from that relationship that I understood how much I was contributing and how little he was. It's a common experience for many people involved with narcissists, and as I've shared my story, I've heard similar tales. The partner is often the one keeping everything together, while the narcissist basks in the limelight as if they were the star of the show.

I've realized I was the perfect source of supply for him. Narcissists are masters of exploiting the people around them, especially those who are hardworking, competent, and willing to go above and beyond. I fit that mold perfectly. I took my responsibilities seriously, I was efficient, and I didn't hesitate to do what was needed to keep things running smoothly. But that's exactly why I became such a valuable target for him. He could sit back, benefit from my work, and yet still make it appear as though he was responsible for all the success. This created the perfect illusion for him, and for a while, I didn't even notice the dynamic.

The truth is that narcissists are emotionally immature and cannot often follow through on their promises. They'll talk a big game, making grand statements about what they can do or what they will accomplish, but when it comes time to actually get things done, they disappear. My husband, Dan, was a classic example of this. As the saying goes, *"Actions speak louder than words."* Narcissists often rely on the power of their words to manipulate situations, but when the moment comes to prove themselves, their lack of action reveals the truth. In my husband's case, he would always boast about what he could achieve, whether it was fixing something around the house or handling a business issue. But when it came time to put those words into practice, he was nowhere to be found.

Chapter 13: Rebuilding Self: Reclaiming My Power

Rebuilding self-esteem is a journey that takes patience and a willingness to explore different approaches. I remember feeling completely lost after a difficult breakup, unsure if I would ever feel like myself again. During this time, I decided to explore different healing practices, which ultimately led me to regain my sense of self-worth. For me, it involved trying out various exercises and techniques, some more effective than others. I used a mix of somatic exercises, personal energy work, and guidance from a spiritual mentor to help me find my way back to a healthier self-perception. Somatic exercises involved physical movement to release stored trauma, personal energy work focused on clearing emotional energy that wasn't mine, and guidance from my spiritual mentor provided insights through tarot and astrology.

One approach that substantially helped me was somatic healing. This is a body-focused practice designed to release trauma stored within the body. I found a practitioner who taught specific exercises that blended yoga and therapeutic movement elements. These exercises were aimed at releasing emotional blockages, and while it was challenging at first, I felt progressively lighter after each session. It wasn't just about stretching or physical movement—it was a way to let go of the negative energy holding me back.

After I went through a particularly tough period, including an arrest, I decided to engage deeply in energy work. With my energy worker, we focused on clearing energy that didn't belong to me—emotions and attachments I had absorbed over time. This process involved acknowledging the different feelings that came up and letting them go. One notable experience was working through my connection with a previous partner. I had this inexplicable sense of connection, almost as if I could feel his thoughts, and it often left me feeling overwhelmed. The minute that I would be feeling that, either he would text me or he would look at my social media like it was clockwork. It was unsettling, as we were not in contact, yet these moments felt synchronized. My energy worker helped me understand that these deep ties stemmed from a repeated pattern across different lifetimes. By releasing that energy, I felt less burdened by emotions that weren't helping me move forward.

My energy worker, Jennifer, also used compassion statements as part of the healing process. This involved looking at either my younger or current self and offering compassion. I would say, 'I'm so sorry that when you were a little girl, you weren't loved how you needed to be loved.' Although I said to myself, these affirmations were directed toward different periods of my life. Much of it was focused on inner child work. In addition, we practiced energy retrieval—taking back energy that belonged to me and returning energy that wasn't mine. This exercise, while somewhat somatic, didn't always involve physical movement. Often, while working alone on the farm, I would talk out loud, stating, 'I retrieve all of my energy from this person,' or 'I return all of their energy chips or control chips.' It was an effective practice for me, done in the privacy of my own space.

In addition to these exercises, I also worked with a spiritual mentor who used tarot and astrology to help me gain insight into my journey. We would meet once a week, and each month, she would provide a combined tarot and astrology reading. This wasn't about predicting the future or looking for magical answers—it was more about offering a different perspective on my experiences. She often mentioned something during a reading that seemed to resonate immediately with what I was going through, even without knowing all the details of my life. These sessions helped me recognize patterns and consider approaching upcoming challenges differently.

On the other hand, the affirmation exercises were initially a bit of a struggle for me. I had a coach who pushed me to do affirmations, but I found them too simplistic and surface-level. It felt disingenuous just to say, "I love myself," without actually addressing the root causes of why I struggled with self-love. Instead, I modified the affirmations to make them more meaningful for me. For example, rather than simply saying, "I am enough," I would remind myself of specific things I had accomplished and why those achievements mattered. This approach gave affirmations more depth and made them feel more real.

While working on rebuilding my self-esteem, I discovered that healing is not linear—it requires continuous attention and adjustment. My spiritual mentor and energy worker often complemented each other's work. Sometimes, something that came up in a tarot session would be something I worked through with my energy worker the following week. It wasn't about quick fixes but about making steady progress and being kind to myself during setbacks.

Rebuilding self-esteem also required setting boundaries. Setting healthy boundaries in relationships has been a major challenge for me. I struggled to express my needs for many years, often prioritizing others' comfort over mine. This habit led to situations where I felt overwhelmed and undervalued. A memorable incident occurred during a massage session that combined chakra alignment and traditional massage techniques. Despite clearly stating my discomfort with leg touch due to extreme ticklishness on the intake forms, the therapist proceeded, causing me anxiety and unease. Instead of addressing my feelings directly, I remained silent, allowing my boundaries to be crossed. This experience showed my difficulty in asserting myself effectively.

Looking back on that day, I realized my inability to set clear boundaries was taking a toll on my well-being. I often found myself fluctuating between being overly accommodating and completely withdrawing. This inconsistency made it difficult for others to understand my limits, leading to frustration. Avoiding confrontation only heightened my discomfort, leaving me dissatisfied and unhappy. It became clear that I needed to change my interaction approach to feel safe and respected.

With Jennifer, I explored the roots of my struggles, tracing them back to my childhood. As the youngest of eight siblings, I often took on a parental role due to my mother's absence. This responsibility taught me to prioritize others' needs over mine, making asserting my limits difficult later in life. Identifying this connection was critical in understanding why I struggled to maintain boundaries. Therapy provided a safe space to delve into these past experiences and begin the process of healing and growth.

Through my sessions with Jennifer, I learned strategies to communicate my needs more effectively. One important lesson was being clear and direct without feeling guilty. I began practicing how to express my discomfort in various situations, starting with less intimidating scenarios. For example, during the massage, I could have firmly requested the therapist to respect my boundaries instead of staying silent. By rehearsing these conversations, I started building the confidence needed to stand up for myself. This practice was essential in gradually changing my behavior and asserting my needs in a healthy manner.

A key moment in my journey was adopting the mindset that setting boundaries is an act of self-respect, not selfishness. Brené Brown once said, *"Daring to set boundaries is about having the courage to love ourselves, even when we risk disappointing others."* This quote rang with me deeply, reinforcing the idea that my needs are just as important as those of others. Embracing this perspective allowed me to prioritize my well-being without feeling guilty. It shifted my understanding of boundaries from negative to positive aspects of self-care and mutual respect in relationships.

Implementing these changes was not without its difficulties. I encountered resistance both within myself and from others. Internally, I battled feelings of guilt and fear of rejection when asserting my boundaries. Externally, some people were unaccustomed to my new assertiveness, leading to misunderstandings and conflicts. However, each challenge strengthened my determination to maintain healthy boundaries. I learned to handle these obstacles by staying consistent and reminding myself of the importance of respectful relationships. Over time, these efforts began to pay off, and I started seeing positive changes in my interactions.

Growing up, I had three sisters and four brothers. My sister Candy, thirteen years older than me, often argued with our mother. The arguments were intense—yelling, crying, and sometimes even slaps. Even though I loved all my siblings, I felt especially connected to Candy. When I was about five, I remember hugging her while she cried. She often confided in me, telling me our mom didn't love her, which broke my heart. I felt responsible, even as a child, to help them reconcile. I would take my mother by the hand

and ask her to make up with Candy. It made me grow up too quickly.

Looking back now, I realize that taking on the role of mediator was not something a child should have to do. My mother and sister's relationship wasn't my responsibility, but as a child, I didn't understand that. I always stepped in, trying to fix things that weren't mine to fix. It's clear to me that my upbringing affected my ability to set boundaries. I learned to take care of others' emotions before my own, which led to deep anxiety that continues to impact me today. The burden of adult responsibility as a child made setting limits feel impossible.

My upbringing taught me to put others first, which has led to problems in my adult life. Even now, I struggle with anxiety about going out alone. When I do try to socialize, I find myself feeling unsafe, especially around men. I want to go out and have fun with my friends, but I often stay home because of my anxiety. Men frequently approach me, and despite my discomfort, I usually give them my number so they will leave me alone. This is not healthy, but it reflects my struggle with boundaries. I want to be firm, but I end up avoiding confrontation.

My relationships as an adult have often mirrored the lack of boundaries I experienced growing up. My husband and a recent boyfriend would tell me I was lucky to have them and that no one else would ever love or want me. Over time, I started to believe those words. The constant belittling damaged my sense of self-worth. When you hear such negativity often enough, you start to internalize it. Today, even when men show interest in me, I question their motives. I think they might be attracted to me, but I doubt if they'll ever truly like who I am. Building self-worth has required ongoing effort. I've had to challenge the negative voices that have echoed in my mind for so long. Self-compassion plays a big role in this process. Positive self-talk has been essential in countering the harmful messages I've heard throughout my life. As I practice being kinder to myself, I remember that my value isn't dependent on whether someone else loves or approves of me. It's an ongoing journey, and I still struggle, but each small step helps me grow stronger and more resilient.

A quote that deeply echoes with me is from Dr. Kristin Neff: *"Self-compassion is giving the same kindness to ourselves that we would give to others."* This reminds me that the empathy I've extended to my sister, my friends, and even strangers is something I deserve to offer myself. Just as I comforted Candy during our turbulent childhood, I need to comfort my heart when self-doubt creeps in. Learning to treat myself with the same care and understanding has been an important part of my healing process.

Setting boundaries has not come easily, but I'm learning. Now, I strive to express my needs clearly, even when uncomfortable. Whether it's telling someone that I'm not interested or choosing to stay home to take care of my mental health, these actions reflect my growing ability to prioritize myself. This process is ongoing, and I know that change won't happen overnight. The scars from my childhood won't disappear easily, but I'm committed to this journey. Every day, I remind myself that I deserve respect and love, starting with self-respect and self-love.

I still have a harsh inner critic, and I'm working on that. Over time, I've explored different hobbies to help me cope. I've always loved yoga and keep returning to it because it helps me feel grounded and centered. I've tried other activities, too, like pole dancing, which was fun but didn't quite resonate with me. Horses have always had a special place in my heart. Being around them brings a sense of calm that nothing else does. Whether riding alone or with friends, horses provide a unique peace. Their presence fills a void I didn't even realize needed filling, and they give me pure joy. Riding and caring for them offers me a sense of connection that I rarely find elsewhere.

Art has also become an important emotional outlet for me. I've returned to it recently, and my paintings reflect what I feel inside. Many of the girls I paint are crying. This recurring theme is something I discussed with Jennifer, who helped me understand its roots. As a child, I never had a safe space to cry. I shared a room with my sister and a bed, and while she tried to comfort me, it never felt quite right. Crying openly was hard, and art became the only way to express those deep emotions. Painting allows me to release the pain I couldn't show when I was young. It's my way of speaking without words, of letting those hidden feelings come to life on canvas. Creating has always been a powerful tool for me to understand myself better.

When I paint, I listen to music, often sad songs, that bring my emotions to the surface. I've noticed that the girls I paint look more like children than adults, and I think it reflects my own childhood experiences. Creating these paintings helps me make sense of the past, offering me a kind of healing. Despite the sadness in my work, painting is comforting. I'm currently working on an Oracle deck, which is a new and exciting project. It gives me purpose and helps me channel my creativity in a meaningful direction, giving me fulfillment. It feels good to work on something that is both expressive and productive, transforming my emotions into something that might one day help others.

I have always extended kindness to others, but now I'm learning to give that same compassion to myself. I'm learning to be patient with myself and that healing takes time. There is no rush to feel completely healed or find the perfect hobby. Every small step I take, whether riding a horse, painting, or practicing yoga, is a part of my journey. Sometimes, my inner critic gets loud, but I am slowly learning to quiet that voice by focusing on what brings me happiness. Growth takes time, and I am committed to the process. It's about progress, not perfection, and embracing each moment for what it is. That's what matters to me now, and I'm finding peace in it. I know that setbacks are part of the journey, but each step forward, no matter how small, is progress.

Chapter 14: Paying It Forward: Becoming an Advocate

The inspiration behind creating an online course, ***"40 Days to Jump Start Your Recovery from Narcissistic Abuse,"*** came from my personal journey. Having gone through several difficult experiences in relationships with narcissists, I reached a point where I sought healing. Throughout my recovery process, I tried various online courses, but many fell short of offering the depth and practical steps I needed to truly heal. This sparked the idea that I could create a more effective course encompassing all the tools and techniques that helped me recover.

Though I cannot pinpoint the exact moment I realized my experiences could benefit others, the gaps in the available resources became evident as I engaged with more courses and remained unfulfilled. Many lacked comprehensive emotional recovery strategies and practical steps to rebuild a life after such traumatic experiences. Having lived through the pain and financial strain of leaving a narcissistic relationship, I understood firsthand the emotional and financial challenges that survivors face. This understanding became central to my motivation to design a course that would be affordable and comprehensive.

A key concept I incorporated into the course is the importance of trauma-informed care. This approach ensures that the course recognizes the lasting effects of abuse and offers a supportive, non-judgmental environment for survivors. Trauma-informed care emphasizes creating safety and empowerment for those in recovery, and I ensured the course reflected this principle. By focusing on emotional safety, survivors can heal without feeling rushed or pressured to achieve specific outcomes, which is critical in recovering from the deep wounds left by narcissistic abuse.

As someone who has been through the cycle of abuse, I know that many people in this situation are often starting from scratch. They've left toxic relationships with very little—emotionally, financially, and in terms of support. I wanted to create a course that could guide rebuilding, offering step-by-step methods I had used successfully in my life.

Another driving force behind the creation of this course was the recognition that every survivor's journey is unique. However, despite the individuality of experiences, there are universal elements in narcissistic abuse—feelings of worthlessness, confusion, emotional exhaustion, and financial instability—that need to be addressed. I designed the course to touch on all of these points, providing a holistic approach to healing that could be adapted to each person's needs.

What also struck me during my journey was the overwhelming amount of information available to survivors. Much of it is scattered across various platforms, making it hard for someone to know where to begin. With this in mind, I wanted to create something cohesive—a single course that would guide someone from the moment they decide to leave an abusive relationship through the long and challenging process of recovery. This course would provide clarity and structure, helping survivors heal without needing multiple, disjointed resources.

The most important aspects of my healing journey start with breaking the trauma bond, which is often one of the hardest but most crucial steps in recovering from narcissistic abuse. Many survivors believe that simply having no contact with the abuser is enough to break free from the trauma bond, but in reality, much deeper work is required. I understood this from my own experience—it's not just about physical separation but about addressing the cognitive dissonance that keeps survivors emotionally tied to their abusers. The first part of the course is dedicated to helping participants recognize and work through this dissonance, which involves untangling the contradictory feelings of love and fear that often plague those recovering from narcissistic relationships.

A significant aspect of my healing process, and thus a key component of the course, was acknowledging the psychological manipulation that kept me attached to the abuser. Narcissists often use tactics like gaslighting, love bombing, and devaluation, which create confusion and self-doubt in their victims. I designed this course to help participants identify these manipulation techniques and understand how they impact their thinking and behavior. The course includes exercises that focus on rebuilding trust in one's perceptions and feelings, helping survivors regain a sense of reality that the abuser's manipulation has distorted.

This allows them to break free not just physically but emotionally and mentally as well, a step that is often overlooked in other recovery programs.

Another key element of the course mirrors my journey by focusing on the importance of self-care and self-compassion. After years of emotional abuse, survivors often have very low self-esteem and may feel undeserving of care or kindness. This course introduces practical self-care techniques early on, not as an afterthought but as a foundational part of the recovery process. Through guided exercises and daily practices, participants learn how to nurture themselves and rebuild their self-worth. This mirrors my path, where learning to care for myself—emotionally, mentally, and physically—was a critical turning point in my healing journey.

The course also incorporates mindfulness and journaling, which were instrumental in my recovery. These tools helped me become more aware of my thoughts and feelings, allowing me to process the trauma in a healthy way. Mindfulness exercises in the course guide participants to stay present and focused on their healing rather than dwelling on the past or worrying about the future. Journaling prompts encourage survivors to express their emotions and reflect on their experiences, which helps break the trauma bond and rebuild emotional resilience. These techniques helped me recognize and release the emotions tied to my abuser, and they are presented in the course as powerful tools for self-reflection and healing.

A unique aspect of the course is its attention to creating a structured recovery plan. In my journey, I found that having a clear roadmap was essential for making progress. Without direction, it's easy to feel overwhelmed and stuck, unsure of what to do next. The course provides a day-by-day guide to recovery, with each day building upon the last, giving survivors a sense of accomplishment and progress. This structure reflects the approach I used during my recovery, where each small victory built upon the previous one, eventually leading to long-term healing and emotional freedom.

Additionally, the course addresses the financial and logistical challenges of recovery. Many survivors are financially strained after leaving an abusive relationship, and expensive therapy or coaching programs may not be feasible. In developing this course, I kept these concerns in mind, offering affordable, practical solutions that provide the same healing benefits without the high costs. This approach mirrors my own experience, where I had to navigate financial challenges while trying to prioritize my emotional well-being. The course is designed to offer effective tools that can be implemented without spending excessive amounts of money on multiple forms of therapy.

Balancing my ongoing personal growth and self-care with my mission to support others on their recovery journey is vital to my work. I know that to truly help others, I must prioritize my health and well-being. One of the most important aspects of maintaining this balance is setting aside time for myself. Just like anyone else, I need to make sure that my emotional, mental, and physical needs are being met. This involves regularly working with my spiritual mentor and energy worker, who have played key roles in my healing process. These practices help me stay grounded and continue healing, which is essential as I guide others through their recovery.

I also recognize the importance of ongoing education, as narcissistic abuse is a constantly evolving area of study. New research, insights, and therapeutic approaches are always emerging, making it essential for me to stay informed. To maintain a high standard of support for my clients, I regularly attend workshops, webinars, and seminars led by leading experts in the field. These learning opportunities deepened my understanding of the subject and provided me with new tools and strategies that I could incorporate into my work. By staying current, I ensure that my guidance is based on the most up-to-date information available, allowing me to offer the most effective and relevant support possible.

In addition to formal education, I actively engage with the latest publications, research papers, and case studies related to narcissistic abuse and trauma recovery. This continuous learning process enables me to refine my approach and stay aware of trends and breakthroughs that could benefit my clients. For example, I recently participated in a specialized workshop that explored new methods for addressing cognitive dissonance in survivors, which I've since integrated into my practice. This commitment to education enhances my knowledge and ensures that I provide my clients with the best possible care tailored to the latest advances in the field.

As the saying goes, *"You need to put your oxygen mask on first before helping others."* This idea is central to how I manage my work. I can't offer the support survivors need unless I am taking care of myself first. My goal is to show up as the best version of myself, which requires constant attention to my growth and well-being. By maintaining a strong foundation in my health, I ensure I have the energy and mental clarity necessary to provide valuable guidance to my clients. It's essential that I model the very self-care practices I encourage survivors to adopt for their healing.

In terms of balance, I've learned that setting boundaries is crucial. Supporting others through their recovery journey can be emotionally draining, and without proper limits, it's easy to burn out. For instance, I allocate specific times during the week for my time—whether it's a quiet morning dedicated to meditation or an afternoon spent outdoors to clear my mind. This structured downtime ensures that I have the mental space needed to recharge so that I can return to my work feeling refreshed and fully present for my clients.

Along with scheduling downtime, I regularly incorporate reflection and personal healing practices into my routine. I take moments to assess my emotional state, ensuring I'm not carrying too much emotional weight from the stories I hear or the guidance I offer. After intense client sessions, I write down my thoughts and emotions, which helps me process them and avoid becoming overwhelmed. This reflective practice keeps me grounded and reinforces my commitment to my mission without sacrificing my well-being.

These boundaries allow me to maintain a healthy work-life balance while giving my clients the attention and support they need. By managing my time effectively and prioritizing my mental health, I ensure that I can continue offering valuable guidance without feeling depleted. For example, I've learned that saying "no" to additional work when feeling stretched is necessary for long-term sustainability. By honoring these boundaries, I protect my well-being and ensure that my help remains genuine and impactful.

Another key aspect of balancing personal growth with supporting others is recognizing that both are interconnected. By continually growing and healing, I become better equipped to guide others on their path. Each new lesson I learn, whether through personal experience or education, becomes a tool I can use to help others. At the same time, helping others often reinforces my healing process, as it reminds me of the progress I've made and the strength I've gained. This reciprocal relationship between personal growth and supporting others allows me to be effective in both areas without sacrificing one for the other.

Lastly, my mission to support others isn't just about teaching or providing resources—it's about nurturing a sense of hope and empowerment in those who are recovering from narcissistic abuse. I need to continue working on my sense of purpose and fulfillment to do that effectively. I bring more passion and energy to my work when I'm engaged in my growth. I can more easily relate to my clients' struggles because I, too, am continually working on myself. This shared experience creates a strong connection between me and those I support, making the recovery journey a collaborative effort rather than a one-sided process.

In essence, balancing my personal growth and self-care with my mission to support others is not only possible but essential. By prioritizing my health, continuing my education, setting boundaries, and recognizing the connection between my growth and my work, I can provide the best support to those on their recovery journey. This balance allows me to be fully present and effective in my mission while ensuring I continue to thrive personally.